THE TWITTER WHO SERIES

A NEW WHOVIAN'S JOURNEY THROUGH CLASSIC TERRITORY 140 CHARACTERS AT A TIME

VOLUME 1: THE FIRST DOCTOR
VOLUME 2: THE SECOND DOCTOR
VOLUME 3: THE THIRD DOCTOR

UPCOMING:

VOLUME 4: THE FOURTH DOCTOR

TWITTER WHO VOLUME 3: THE THIRD DOCTOR

RAGGEDY MOON BOOKS

TWITTER WHO VOLUME 3: THE THIRD DOCTOR

2015
Raggedy Moon Books

Cover design by Hannah J. Rothman
hannahjrothman.com

Book interior design by Faith L. Justice
faithljustice.com

ISBN: 0692568549
ISBN-13: 978-0692568545

Raggedy Moon Books
Brooklyn, NY, USA
raggedymoonbooks.com

CONTENTS

Introduction
Season 7
With Liz Shaw

Season 8
With Jo Grant

Season 9

Season 10

Season 11
With Sarah Jane

About the Author

ACKNOWLEDGEMENTS

Special thanks to Stephen Fry, for whom I got on Twitter in the first place; Toria, whose live-Tweeting of "The End of Time, Part 2" made me want to give it a shot as well; Dave, who actually got me watching the show and graciously supplied the DVDs of seasons 1-4 for our weekly marathons; all my Whovian friends on Tumblr, especially the loving and supportive circle of the TPC with whom I became active in fandom like never before; Mom, who pointed to my blog and reminded me that I had quite a bit of material there that I could do something with.

Twitter Who Volume 3: The Third Doctor

Hannah J. Rothman

INTRODUCTION

One of the things that first attracted me to Doctor Who was the presence and meaning of the TARDIS. It filled a gap that other Wandering the Earth/Universe stories usually left empty: a home base. The one TV show I would arguably cite as being my favorite of all time, just one slot above Doctor Who, is Samurai Jack. Like the Doctor, Jack traveled around the world fighting evil, helping people, and generally being a moral center everywhere he went. But Jack didn't have a home anymore. He was a man out of time (long story short, he had a nemesis with the power to control time portals) and lived in a dystopian future that was not his own. There was even an entire episode where he finds the ruins of the city in Japan where he spent his childhood, and it was one of the saddest things ten-year-old me had ever seen. Jack and the Doctor are both constant wanderers, but where Jack kept on traveling, the Doctor made a new home for himself when he left Gallifrey. That was the TARDIS.

So what happens when the Doctor basically loses his self-made home as well? We get the Third Doctor era and the UNIT Family. I do understand that the constant flow of Earth stories can get under a lot of people's skin, but speaking as someone who joined Doctor Who long after that era ended, I saw it as more of a fun curiosity. The Doctor doesn't have just one companion; he has a whole team of new partners who have his back, each one glowing with personality. Yes, while Liz Shaw, Jo Grant, and Sarah Jane Smith are the ones always cited as "the Third Doctor's companions," the UNIT boys are not to be overlooked either. Especially since, counting Harry Sullivan in the first Tom Baker season, UNIT is the last source of male companions or recurring supporting characters for a good several seasons. The Third Doctor era gave us a combination of elements that no other era of the show had: a single non-TARDIS base of operations, and a larger secondary cast. This made UNIT HQ almost feel like home, although we don't see that much of it beyond the Doctor's lab and the Brigadier's office. It was always the place to come back to.

Although, I find it kind of interesting that an era where the folks in charge were afraid of people being driven away by repetition was the one that produced the Whole Season of the Master. My character retrospective for the Master will come in a later volume, since his tenure on the show is fairly erratic (especially when Anthony Ainley takes over and starts only showing up about once or twice per Doctor). But he remains hands down my favorite villain on the whole show and I think that Roger Delgado did him a damn near perfect introduction. Giving the Doctor a nemesis who was a single character, as opposed to the Daleks and Cybermen which were both villainous races, was certainly a welcome addition to the fold. There are a lot of favorites to be had in this era: introduction of my favorite villain, my favorite multi-Doctor story, many favorite characters, and the grand confession: when asked, "who's your favorite Classic Doctor?" my go-to answer is "Jon Pertwee."

—Hannah J. Rothman

SPEARHEAD FROM SPACE

Written by Robert Holmes
Aired: January 3 – 24 1970

SPEARHEAD FROM SPACE! FIRST ADVENTURE OF THE THIRD DOCTOR! AND IT'S FINALLY IN COLOR!

The TARDIS lands, and Three...just falls out. Okay......HEY THAT MUST BE LIZ SHAW.

So they found him and took him to a hospital? How did they even DO that?

Wait a sec...when did Two meet UNIT before? *checks Wikipedia*

Ah, The Web of Fear. Okay, sense of making now.

Oh snap. When the internets said Two became Three through a forced regeneration, they weren't kidding.

That guy in the phone booth kinda looks like an older John Simm...

"How are you feeling, sir?"
"SHOES."
I'm not sure whether to find this funny or wait for Three to act less senile.

"Are these what you're looking for?"
GRAB *shoe-cuddle*

"...maybe the brain's damaged."
I'm sorry, that was hilarious.

Sneaky Doctor, hiding the TARDIS key in his shoe...

OH SHIT HE'S BEING ABDUCTED WHAT

HOLY SHIT HE'S ESCAPING BY WHEELCHAIR OH MY
GOD THREE IS FUCKING AMAZING

WHAT THE FUCK WHERE DID ALL THOSE DEAD PLASTIC
BABY HEADS COME FROM OH MY GOD THAT WAS
"BLINK"-LEVEL OF CREEPY

Sorry for all of the all-caps but...seriously, holy shit.

Oh wait, it's just a doll factory. OH WAIT MAYBE THESE GUYS
ARE AUTONS.

Yeah. That woman's face is way too shiny.

"A man who travels through time and space in a police box?" I think
I love Liz Shaw just for that one line.

Okay, THAT was an Auton.

So of COURSE he ducks into the room labeled "Doctors Only."
That. brilliant. wow.

Woah. Wait. Three in shower. What. No. We do not need to see this.

He showered with his watch on. And he has a tattoo on his right arm.
And I still can't quite grasp what constitutes as "weird" on this show.

That is a really old-school car. What decade does this take place in?

That's a surprising amount of blood they just showed...

Originally Posted February 3rd, 2010

The Silurians

Written by Malcolm Hulke
Aired: January 31 – March 14, 1970

Oh, Three's titles, how long has it been since I saw you?

Miners in a mine hear a strange noise. Gee, I wonder where this could possibly be going.

Rubber Suit Monster: 1, Miners: 0.

And we return to UNIT HQ with Three singing The Jabberwocky and UNEXPECTED CROTCH SHOT HELLO

"Miss Shaw, I never report myself anywhere. Particularly not forth-with!"

Wait. This is the serial right after Spearhead From Space...so Three and Liz have only known each other HOW long? They seem pretty matey.

Bessie's maiden voyage! And does anyone else find it weird that Liz convinced Three to come out because of "the caves"? Clearly I'm twelve.

"Ah, there you are at last!"
"There YOU are at last!"
HELLO BRIG.

If the Brig keeps talking to the Doctor like a bothersome child, I will be laughing forever.

Also, short skirts: Liz wears them. I'm surprised that the Classic companions' wardrobes are still surprising me.

I think that's the first time in anything I've ever seen somebody go from drawing on the wall to strangling someone. And Three fends him off

"He's just frightened, that's all."
"So was I. What's made him like this?"
"Some kind of fear."
GEE YA THINK.

Jeez. What IS it with people going crazy and strangling other people in this story?

Apparently Time Lords adopt red ascots as part of their cave-going gear.

Ah, that old-school middle-eight. Haven't heard that in a while...

Rubber Suit Monster: 0, Doctor: 1, even though he didn't even do anything.

"Could it have been prehistoric?"
"Well, it was certainly some kind of dinosaur..."

"That's typical of the military mind, isn't it? Present them with a new problem and they start shooting at it!"

Rubber Suit Monster: 1, UNIT: 0.

Apparently the Silurians see in red-triangle vision.

So if the Silurians have been established as reptilian, how can they still be so active without sunlight?

So green means "item get" and red means "mind control"?

"Get on to the police! Tell them there's something in my barn!"
"What sort of something?"
Something that's probably going to attack you.

"Is he qualified to make such an investigation?"

"The Doctor is qualified to do almost everything."
Note that he didn't say "anything."

Wow. Three is quite a speed-artist. So is Pertwee, apparently, considering how fast the pen's moving. Unless Pertwee's just scribbling.

OH CRAP NOT LIZ. Also, these cliffhangers don't feel the same without the electronic screech to accompany them.

Guys, I do not understand what the music is doing right now. It sounds like it's dreaming of being at a haunted party naked. #descriptionwin

Okay, so you're just going to knock Liz over and consider making a run for it? Okay...

Three/Liz is quickly becoming an OTP. I've already reached the point where I can't look at them and NOT go "d'aaaaaaaaaawwwwww..."

Also, I decided to turn InfoText on, just for the fun of it.

It's certainly interesting, but also really distracting. Maybe I should turn it off. Also, WINDOW PERTWEE.

Unless I'm mistaken, that's a prehistoric globe Liz is holding.

I AM NOT MISTAKEN. *glares at Earthshock*

Annoyed Three is annoyed at interrupting!Brigadier.

Complete with facepalming.

It amuses me a little more than it should that this episode ended with Three's WHAT-face.

extends hand "Hello. Are you a Silurian?" Oh Doctor...

Always the diplomat. Also, wow: Silurians = cannot take seriously. This should NOT surprise me at ALL.

Silurians: 1, UNIT: 0.

Is it just me, or is Liz wearing a shorter skirt than before? Also, Three seems to have become fond of double-facepalming.

Fake caves are fake. According to the InfoText, these scenes were supposed to be shot in real caves, but they were too far from London.

"Well you can't without one of those things that it was carrying."
"Yes, of course!"
"I suppose you just HAPPEN to have one in your pocket?"

So of COURSE the Silurians can't hear our protagonist's unusually loud whispering.

Looks like the Doctor's "attack an alien and it'll hate humans" mantra is ringing true here.

Wow. The Silurian's third red eye is certainly quite a multi-purpose little bugger.

I'm no expert on prehistorical dialects, but I'd almost say that one of those Silurians has the reptilian equivalent of an American accent.

The origin of the moon according to Doctor Who: a "small planet" neared Earth, drove the Silurians underground, and got pulled into orbit.

"Would your people agree to this?"
"Well, they're not my people."
Strange how easy it is for me to forget that the Doctor isn't human.

When your team is about to die of oxygen deprivation, someone hyperventilating and doodling on the wall probably isn't the best thing.

"When the apes used to raid our crops..." Wait, I thought you guys were long gone before apes evolved?

Guys, this music really bugs me. It sounds like an electronic clown is laughing musically at me. #moredescriptionwin

"The Brigadier and the Doctor are risking their LIVES trying to solve your problems."
"That's a matter of opinion."
BURN.

And now this piece of music sounds like "Taps" except...not.

"Major Baker...you are ill. You are very very ill." Um. Three. He's infected with a DEADLY BACTERIA. WHY ARE YOU TAKING YOUR TIME WITH THIS.

Don't you think it's kind of unfair for a species to evolve an appendage that SHOOTS INVISIBLE DEATH RAYS?

So Masters was played by Geoffrey Palmer! One of Those British Guys whose names I know but whose works I can't identify...

Huh. For just a few seconds at the beginning of this ep, I could see the faint "ghost" of the end credit reading "Doctor Who: Jon Pertwee."

Also, dead Major Baker is dead.

Is laboratory tiems nao.

Turned on the InfoText again out of curiosity. It has a "don't try this at home" disclaimer for Liz giving Three an injection.

There's that "credit ghost" again...

Oh BALLS. Nearly everybody who came in contact with Baker is sick, and now Masters has caught it and is BACK IN LONDON.

I actually cringe just a little bit every time he gets NEAR anybody.

Even the Silurians have picked up on the turn-and-speak-to-the-camera gimmick.

"At this time, Doctor Who serials were deemed to be set roughly ten years in the future." Unit Dating Controversy: Solved.*

Uh oh, now the ticket man at the train station is collapsing.

Now EVERYBODY AT THE STATION IS GOING DOWN. I love the sense of scale we're starting to get here. (No pun intended)

Obviously whoever wrote the InfoText has a sense of humor. They refer to "copies of The Times and other less exalted newspapers."

"I'm beginning to lose confidence for the first time in my life. And that covers several thousand years." WHAT.

I've heard the Doctor's age gradually increase in hundreds over the years but...THOUSANDS? That's just not right. Two said he was about 450.

And the InfoText makes note of this. Good.

Okay, Dr. Lawrence just has no good sense at all. He's DYING for Christ-sake and he's STILL accusing the Brig of a conspiracy.

Also, uh oh, looks like Three isn't "fine" anymore...

WOW. InfoText tells me there was some unintentional Enforced Method Acting going on that resulted in Lawrence's rage being a RAGE-SPLOSION.

FOUND CURE HAS BEEN FOUND.

Okay, seriously, this is the THIRD episode this serial that's ended with Three's WHAT-face. THE SITUATION IS DIRE. WE GET IT.

About a Radio Times photoshoot: "Between official shots, Pertwee clowned around as a Silurian-headed Doctor."

"With inspired lunacy, he then became a flat-capped Silurian-headed Doctor."

Doctor-dragging Okay...seriously...he didn't HEAR THEM BURN THROUGH THE WALL AND WALK UP BEHIND HIM?

Okay, so my eyes are scarred forever by Pertwee-in-shower, but Pertwee-with-tight-tshirt makes me GUH a little bit. What the hell, brain?

Wow. So after all that ambition and killing his own leader, that one Silurian is volunteering to die to save his own people.

I wish I could come up with a clever portmanteau of "Pertwee" and "tattoo" to refer to a certain dragon on his arm.

Is that an early hint of neutron flow I hear? "Pertwee found the phrase memorable because he realized that he could sing it to the tune of 'When I Was a Lad' from Gilbert and Sullivan's HMS Pinafore." I'll have to look that up later.

And the Silurian base goes "s'plody." Not happy Doctor is not happy. I think I spent too much of the past few episodes reporting on the InfoText and not the actual episodes. I'll try to monitor that better.

Sorry about that, but since I'm not watching many of these on DVD it shouldn't be a major recurring problem.

Also I should point out that I refuse to call this story "Doctor Who and the Silurians." For reasons. That I have.

*Despite this, I still used the Present Day tag for this episode for several reasons: One, the date is never explicitly stated in the actual episode. Two, the date suggested by the InfoText still falls within the range of Classic Who airdates (between 1963 and 1989). Three, the environment is still perfectly passable as the time in which it was shot and aired, especially with all the on-location shooting in London.

Wibbly-wobbly timey-wimey. It gets a little frustrating sometimes.

Originally Posted May 26th, 2010

THE AMBASSADORS OF DEATH

Written by David Whitaker, Trevor Ray, Terrance Dicks, and Malcolm Hulke
Aired: March 21 – May 2, 1970

Wow. Never seen a Pertwee title done like THAT before. Opening credits, then teaser clip, THEN the story title.

Not to mention the OVER-DRAMATIC MUSIC!

I've also never seen a TARDIS interior like that before; it looks like an actual room! Complete with TV!

Wait now it's teleporting individual people and what?

So I don't understand how one ship is in color and the other ship is in black and white.

"What do you mean, you can't remember?"
"Don't you understand? It's all up here in my mind. The information's here but I can't REACH it!"

By the way, how is it that Jon Pertwee always got the Doctor's spiffiest outfits EVER?

"My dear fellow, I simply don't happen to HAVE a pass! ...Because I don't believe in them, that's why!" Because he's the DOCTOR, that's why!

Liz speaks French! You learn something new every day.

These guys in the warehouse are managing to take out fully-armed UNIT agents with HANDGUNS. Impressive.

"You kill me, my men kill you." The Brig > all of you.

I've been putting the UNIT stories under the Present Day tag on the Blog, but the technology in this story is making that less believable.

So apparently they've decided that Athens is a major space center in the '70s version of the '80s. Interesting choice.

That was an unusually abrupt cliffhanger: Three and Liz enter the computer room and within 5 seconds MAN WITH GUN!

The Doctor and his magic tiemfingers MAKE TAPES DISAPPEAR!

"Where is the tape?"
"Perhaps he sent it into the future."
Aaaaand, CUE INCOMING-BRIG!

When did the Doctor magically gain the ability to dematerialize objects WITH HIS FINGERS?

"Have a cup of tea?"
"Yes, thanks!"
"That's good...STANDTOATTENTIONWHENYOU'RETALKIN GTOMEANDCALLME'SIR'!"
"SIR!"

"There has been another extraordinary development in the mystery of Mars Probe 7." Indeed there is. The color just went away.

For some reason, it's weirder hearing Pertwee's voice with the black and white instead of actually SEEING him in black and white.

Wow. The Brigstache looks remarkably greyer in black and white.

Color's back! I know that a handful of Pertwee episodes only exist in black and white, so I won't be surprised when they come up.

All of the driving sequences in this story are accompanied by such pretty music...

Random helicopter! And why is that one guy wearing a metal Hannibal Lector mask?

G-AWFLCOPTER!

Jesus, they've got people flying helicopters and flying of motorcycles, how'd they do all the stuntOH MY GOD THEY SHOT THE BRIG.

So it looks like thanks to car trouble with Bessie, Three missed all the action.

Color's gone again...

"Well, if you want me to get out of the way, I'm afraid you'll have to help me?" Oh my god, please tell me there is impending Time Fu...

Guess not. And apparently Bessie's anti-theft device makes people STICK TO HER. "Don't worry, it'll switch itself off. Eventually."

And the Brig is magically fine. And you know why? Because THE BRIG.

"Didn't you find two angry men stuck to my car?"
"No, just the car."

I've noticed that the bad guys in this story have a kind of jazzy James-Bond-like leitmotif. Interesting choice.

The ending credits look interesting in black and white.

Nice hat, Liz.

They keep cutting back and forth between the bodies being dumped into the quarry and the gravel going up the conveyor belt. Big claw is big.

Wow. Impressive car. It can flip its license plates AND change its company banner.

Geez, it seems like EVERYBODY in power is in on this weird plot.

"Isotopes? Well, you'd better get them over here." Whait oh no where id isotop? #yayforobscurefanfictionreferences

Huh. I'm surprised that Three is letting Liz drive Bessie on her own. Then again, she IS a companion...

Somehow I had a feeling that this was going to be resolved (for the moment) by her flipping over the railing into the water.

Ah, the opening sequence in black and white. Let's see if I can still pick out the color changes...

And I can, to an extent.

I'm only just now realizing how '70s Liz's outfit is. Or was it the '80s...

Wait, Dr. Taltalian had a GUN trained on Three a few episodes ago and now he's okay to work with? What?

"They have found her?"
"No, someone's threatening to kill her if I don't stop interfering. Well, let's get back to work, shall we?"
LIZ NOOO

So Liz tries hitchhiking away from the baddie base and JUST HAPPENS to be picked up by Taltalian. WHAT ARE THE ODDS? *rimshot*

Looks like the "kill the Doctor with an exploding briefcase" ploy didn't work either.

I don't think they've said if Taltalian was dead or not, but Three gets away from the blast with just a bandage on his cheek. Nice.

Three, please ignore the body and notice the walking radioactive spacesuit that's about to kill you.

Wow. Most conveniently-timed Brigadier EVER.

Wait...BENTON WAS THAT YOU JUST NOW?

Dr. Lenox, you might want to do something about your hair. It's kinda EVERYWHERE.

Benton! It is you! This must be your debut story.

"Hello, Brigadier. What brings you here?"
"Thought I'd see you off."
Aww, he does care...

Oh wait a sec, Benton was in The Invasion too, so this wouldn't be his debut story.

Also, Reegan is a freaking ACROBAT.

Whait oh no there id isotop!

Bored Doctor is bored. Also, will disastrous space launch be disastrous?

Yes, but only for a few minutes. Lack of music prompted me to add Corridors and Fire Escapes which worked quite well.

And now Three has, what appears to be, a giant floating space vagina about to crash into his ship.

More black and white titles!

Color's back. And looks like we're FINALLY about to see what the Ambassadors really are. Three said earlier that they sounded familiar...

Well, there's the three astronauts at last! They seem to be having the time of their lives.

So THAT'S what they look like. Kinda like Predator, but silver.

NO WAIT *THAT'S* WHAT THEY REALLY LOOK LIKE OH MY GOD THEY'RE ALMOST LIKE WALKING CORPSES.

I wonder what Reegan put on that notepad to make the guard let a bakery truck into a space command facility.

Pertwee in a bathrobe! Let's just hope we don't have to watch him taking a shower again.

Oh uh, gassed Three is gassed!

"Your Doctor friend's as dead as a doornail." Except he's not. Immune to death as the plot demands, remember?

I've said it before and I'll say it again: I really love seeing Three and Liz together. Such a shame their time together was so short.

Two cliffhangers with the Doctor facing a gun in one serial? That has to be a record.

The ambassadors' leitmotif started really annoying me quite some time ago...

Crafty Doctor with his Morse SOS signal is crafty.

And awesome escaping!Brig is awesome.

And he even gets to drive Bessie!

"What kept you?"
"I see YOU'RE alright, Doctor. Miss Shaw?"
"Just get me out of here."

So we don't actually get to see the ambassador/astronaut exchange, but we are left to assume that it happened.

Originally Posted July 19th, 2010

INFERNO

Written by Don Houghton
Aired: May 9 – June 20, 1970

HOLY SHIT. THE TITLES. ON TOP OF
VOLCANOES. AND LAVA. AND S'PLOSIONS.
ASFHKLADSHFKLDSHFKLDSHFKLSD

I wonder what song Three is singing...uh oh, green goop bubbling
out of the floors is usually never a good thing...

Green Goop Guy (Slocum, who kinda looks like Richard Pryor)
growling and attacking people...that can't be good either...

Oh, hello again, Benton! You know, I think it's time I gave you a Tag
on the Blog.

Brig does not approve of Benton laughing at his old military photos.
It's okay if the Doctor does it, though.

That woman's name is Petra? We're using pun names now?

So I was wrong about the TARDIS interior in Ambassadors. He's
taken the console OUT of the TARDIS entirely. Wonder how he did
that.

Oh my god. Three just got trapped in that weird flashing-faces
sequence from the end of 2001: A Space Odyssey.

I'm not even going to bother mentioning the impracticality of Liz's insanely short skirt in this serial. Oh wait...

I'm sensing more and more potential romantic interest between Mr. Sutton and Petra. It just seems to happen when a man and woman argue alot.

So Three recognizes the growling sound from Krakatoa? You know, I used to think that was what Jamie said when he screamed "Creag an tuire!"

"Yes, well I'll tell you something that should be of vital interest to you, professor."
"About what?"
"YOU, sir, are a NITWIT!"

EVERY time a main antagonist comes into contact with a dangerous substance and says he's fine, he NEVER is.

See? First Marsters in The Silurians, now Professor Stahlman here.

"DOCTOR! What do you think you're doing?!?"
"Venusian Karate."
TIME-FU!

And according to the InfoText it was originally meant to be Martian Karate. I like what they stuck with. It's more unique and sounds neater.

And off goes Three, taking Bessie with him, into thin air...

CAR CHASE! And he's got alter-verse UNIT peoples shooting at him. Including Benton.

Woah. Nice haircut, other-Liz.

And she's even got red tinge in her hair for some reason. She almost looks like an adult evil version of Susan.

They're certainly using a lot of shots of people's legs in this sequeOH HAI EVIL!BRIG!

"Look, your name IS Lethbridge-Stewart?"
"Yes."
"Brigadier Lethbridge-Stewart?"
"Brigade Leader."

Guys, I'm a bit blown away by Nicholas Courtney's acting chops here. The differences in nuance between the Brig and the Leader are AMAZING.

So it looks like the Professor in this universe is being plagued by the green goop as well. Funny how things work out that way.

"I don't exist in this world!"
"Then you won't feel the bullets when we shoot you."

@ThirdDoctor I just saw you take out an alternate universe Sergeant Benton with two fingers. Very awesome, sir.

Everyone's suddenly becoming strangely more cooperative with Three. Maybe crises just do that to people.

"Whatever they've taught you in this bigoted world, you've still got a mind of your own. Now USE IT!"

Huh. I'd always thought that brown patch on the side of Jon Pertwee's hair was a trick of the light, but it looks pretty brown to me here.

Oh god. They've got Three under the interrogation lamp and everything.

So I wonder who the person sleeping under the blanket is. I bet we won't find out until the cliffhanger.

"Oh, go away and give me some peace."
"When I say get on your feet, prisoner, I mean GET ON YOUR FEET!"
"Oh, well that's different."

"(The shift from Warp to Warp is represented by a silvered drum revolving on a vertical axis.)" In other words, a disco ball?

Okay, so I was wrong about the reveal waiting until the cliffhanger. But that thing's trying to kill Benton o_o

AND IT CAN BEND METAL BARS. Which it can apparently only do to get INto Three's cell, but not to get out of it.

Wait, so why isn't it until RIGHT before Penetration Zero that Three suddenly tries to stop the whole operation?

And despite all the insane craziness, Three still calls him "Brigadier."
And he responds. Aww...

They've still got about 2 1/2 episodes left, and yet this feels very
much like a climax to me. The alternate world is going up in flames...

Looks like the alternate Sutton and Petra are finally getting together.
Alter-Called it.

Evil!Brig and the other Liz want to go with Three to save their skins,
but WILL IT TAKE OFF?

BLUE LION PEOPLE!

"BENTON, GET OUUUUT!" Oh crap, I don't see this ending
well...

Then again, there's SO MUCH that happens in this story that I can't
see ending well.

Yikes. Benton transformed FAST.

Uh oh, looks like Sir Keith dies in both worlds in an auto accident
anyway. Ouch.

Has anyone else noticed that this facility seems to have the most
conveniently-placed fire extinguishers EVER?

I mean, it seems like there's ALWAYS one RIGHT THERE
whenever Three needs one.

"But there ARE other fire extinguishers at Central Control!" Yes, and
one RIGHT BEHIND YOU, apparently.

"Says he's too busy to,"
"To busy to what, Sergeant?"
"He says he's too busy to waste time bandying words with a pompous
military idiot, sir"

Yikes. Regular!Brig is starting to sound a lot like Evil!Brig.

Three just made a Batman reference. Where did that come from.

Also, I'm impressed with Petra for summing up the nerve to tell off
Evil!Brig for making unreasonable demands of her.

So the reactor switch isn't working and the monsters are closing in. Also, LOTS of s'plosions. This is looking extremely very not good.

Oh wow. I think Evil!Brig is finally starting to have his Villainous Breakdown. And Sutton is taking this BEAUTIFULLY well.

FIGHT FIGHT FIGHT FIGHT FIGHT FIGHT. AND SUTTON'S WINNING.

Holy motherfreaking crap. They're literally showing doomsday here. I'm not sure if I'm tearing up from the tragedy or the lack of blinking.

Just one more episode and this remarkably epic chapter comes to a fiery close...

Wait...Three's suddenly lying unconscious alone on the floor next to the console and...please tell me it wasn't all just a dream...

Okay, if Liz and Benton see him back after being missing, then I guess it all did really happen.

I'm assuming that strange ringing sound was the "sound of the Earth screaming" that Three referenced a couple episodes ago.

"I'll send for a doctor."
"I happen to BE a doctor, Brigadier, remember?"
Oh Liz, I'm gonna miss you.

And Petra and Sutton seem to be on the verge of confessing some feelings for each other. Called it, again.

"How are you, Doctor?"
"Fine, Brigadier. You know, you really do look better with that mustache."
"Delirious, poor chap..."

So they've stopped the drill in our world, but the episode's only half done. I wonder if he finds a way to save the other world...

Our Sir Keith lives! He just got away with a broken arm!

I think Three is giving us the Classic equivalent of the "time can be rewritten" revelation right now.

And he acts on it by smashing things with a wrench. *inches away slowly...*

"We have no PROOF of an emergency situation!" I'd say the boss showing up as a lava mutant is perfectly acceptable proof.

50 SECONDS TO SAVE THE WORLD.

Finished with 35 SECONDS TO SPARE! THREE/LIZ HUG! 2,000TH TWEET SINCE MY UNEXPLAINED RESET LAST MONTH!

"Goodbye, Brigadier!"
"Oh, there's quite a lot of mopping up to do! I shall be around for quite a while yet..."
"Oh, pity."

Uh oh. Three is MAD, and I don't see this TARDIS take-off ending well...

"Goodbye, Liz. I shall miss you, my dear, but I've had about all I can stand of this POMPOUS SELF-OPINIONATED IDIOT HERE."

Actually, that ended quite comically. Apparently, Three accidentally landed the TARDIS console in a dump a few hundred yards away.

They never did explain what that green goop was or how it did what it did to all the mutants, did they...

And we end Jon Pertwee's first season with joking-Doctor, smug-Brig and a final shot of laughing-Liz. Goodbye, Miss Shaw. We hardly knew ye.

Originally Posted July 21st, 2010

CHARACTER RETROSPECTIVE: LIZ SHAW

For every Whovian, I think, there exists a list of sorely underrated characters. Sitting high with the best of mine is one Elizabeth Shaw. Liz is, quite simply, great. It would almost be enough for me to say she's a smart, independent, professional woman who don't take no guff. But that's not quite enough. Actually, (from what I understand), for the Powers That Be of the time, it was too much. Liz Shaw is presented as almost the Doctor's equal, or at least as close as a human companion could be. She's sharp as a tack, immensely intelligent, quick-thinking, able to hold her own, and knows her worth. She's able to complete Three's unfinished projects, rescue herself, and keep a level head in tense situations.

We regularly talk about one-off characters whom we wish could become companions, like Sally Sparrow from "Blink," and I think Liz is the like the full realization of Anne Travers from "The Web of Fear." She is the nonchalant conviction of "when I was a little girl I thought I'd like to become a scientist, so I became a scientist" personified (one of my followers mentioned their surprise that I didn't include that line when I did that commentary, so I intend to rectify that here). Coming at the very beginning of the UNIT era, I think it's actually pretty important that the Doctor have a companion like her. A recurring conflict, especially in "The Silurians," is the issue of UNIT tending to shoot first and ask questions later. With the Third Doctor attempting to settle into this environment, having a respected fellow scientific mind at his side probably helped make that transition a bit easier.

Unfortunately, it seems like one of the defining aspects of Liz Shaw's time on the show is how short it is. It helps that three of her only four stories are quite lengthy, but in the end it still only adds up to four. Liz is a well of could-have-beens. She has all this fantastic capability that she gets to show off on Earth, and it's really a shame that we never get to see her apply these talents to adventures in space or on alien worlds. How would Liz react to going up against the Daleks, or the Cybermen? How would her character change or develop?

One of Liz's only shortcomings, and I use the word very loosely here, is the fact that her limited tenure doesn't allow for much character growth. But on the other hand, she comes across as so complete a character that she almost doesn't need it. The big change she does make over the course of season 7 is a shift in her worldview. She maintains a healthy dose of skepticism and doesn't suspend disbelief throughout most of the beginning of "Spearhead from Space," but comes around to the strange reality of the situation quite promptly when the need arises. On the other hand, this development is far from unique in the world of *Doctor Who*.

In the end, Liz Shaw left me wanting more, in the good way. I wanted her on for another season. I wanted to know more about her. What was her childhood like? What inspired her to go into science? What exactly was she studying at Cambridge when UNIT called her in? Most importantly, why exactly did she leave? We know why Caroline John left, but where did Dr. Elizabeth Shaw go?

TERROR OF THE AUTONS

Written by Robert Holmes
Aired: January 2-23, 1971

An Auton story opening at the circus? Gee, I don't see this ending badly at ALL.

OH HELLO MAGICALLY APPEARING TRUCK THAT SOUNDS LIKE A TARDIS.

And he just jumps out the back door and strolls away like nothing. Ladies and gentlemen: the one, the only, the diabolical, the Master.

"Who the heck are you?" What the heck is your accent?

"I am usually referred to as the Master."
"Oh, is that so?"
"Universally."

So, I have to admit, this is a much less ceremonious introduction than I would expect for such a major character.

Wow. He didn't even have to use a "you will obey me" on him. And why did that guard need a bluescreened background for that one shot?

"Iiiii didn't meeeean to set the woooorld on fiiirrrrre...OFFF"
boom

Three! It's been a long time! And who's that at the door? JO GRANT! Haven't seen you since...well...Death of the Doctor!

"...this area is strictly out of bounds to everybody except the tea lady and the Brigadier's personal staff?"
"I'm your new assistant!"

I'll bet Jo is the only new companion to come right up to the Doctor and tell him in as many words to his face. Awesome.

Well, at least we've got the Autons identified right off the bat.

Meanwhile, atop a radio tower, SCIENCE!

I'll bet that was the first use of the Master's TCE. I have to admit, it looked less phallic back in the '70s.

Ack, closeup of the Nestene sphere reveals, like many things on this show, production shoddiness. Balls. I liked that prop.

BRIIIIIIIIIIIIIIIIIIIIIIIIIIIIIIIIIIIIIIIIIG!

"What you need Doctor as Miss Shaw herself so often remarked is someone to pass you your test tubes, and to tell you how brilliant you are."

Things I've missed lately: that smug look the Brig gives the Doctor when he knows he's right.

Ooo, first mention of Yates! I wonder if we'll get to meet him this episode?

Ah, there he is! Hello, Yates!

So right when I'm thinking "oh wait, The Time Warrior was the last Three serial I watched and that was this spring..." what.

No seriously. I think the Master's TARDIS just materialized as...a... dude...with...a cane...in mid-air...what.

Unless...that's...another Time Lord...? What?

Ah, so it is. Three hears the Master's on the loose and all he says is "that jackanapes, all he ever does is cause trouble!" UNDERSTATE-MENT.

"He's a...he's an unimaginative plodder!"
"His degree in cosmic science was of a higher class...than yours."
#oooburn

Wow. Whoever this Time Lord is, he seems to be present solely for the purpose of smug mockery towards Three.

And I don't mean that in the nice fun Brigly way, either.

This has been another edition of Oh So That's Where That Gif Came From!

Oh wow. With Ainley they always made little models of the TCE victims, but here they're actually showing the scaled-down actors.

"I thought you took an A-level in science."
"Didn't say I passed."

Ah, THERE'S our "you will obey me."

Jo, I think you're in trouble now.

I really hope Jo gets out of that hypnosis soon, because this really isn't a good way to introduce a new companion.

On a lighter note, BENTON!

Aaaand suddenly the two company execs are arguing over the place as a family business. Okay.

Okay seriously what's up with all the greenscreened backgrounds in this episode? Was the budget so low they couldn't afford studio shots?

Did...Jo just punch Yates in the stomach? Yes, I think she did. That would be awesome if she wasn't doing it For Evil.

I was going to mention this in the first ep, but the music they're using is the Second Doctor's theme. I thought they'd shortened it by now?

Aaaaaand UNIT HQ is conveniently next to a bay into which Three can throw the bomb. Well. That was handy. Hi, seagulls.

An unfortunate pitfall of Classic Who: at the right angle, you can very clearly see that the TARDIS prop is completely empty.

"This plastic has got unique properties." Like MURRRRRDEEEEEERRRR.

Oh god. Especially with that music, that is a VERY sinister armchair. Holy crap.

"Try sitting in it." AND I THINK WE ALL KNOW HOW THIS IS GOING TO END.

And the children of Britain never sat in plastic chairs, or slept, ever again. #omnomnom

I'm surprised Three is just talking to Jo to revive her instead of using one of his Time Lord mind powers.

Family business time, and now we've brought in Daddy!

Looks like he also comes equipped with +5 immunity against hypnosis.

Unfortunately that won't stop the Master from throwing the creepiest troll doll ever into the back of his car.

Awww, at least Three's quick to forgive Jo for the whole s'plosion fiasco.

"You know, Brigadier, your methods have all the refined subtlety of a bull in a china shop." This bickering will never get old. Ever.

............why is there a blowfish hanging from the ceiling.

Did Yates just say "what's up, then?" in a playful and possibly-hitting-on-Jo kind of way? Okay.

Evil plastic trolls are heat-activated, apparently.

Ohhhhhhhh Master you cheeky cheeky bastard. You were three steps ahead this whole time instead of just one.

Awww, elephants :D

Suddenly, completely-expected-Jo!

"There's something...evil about it." ACK, DON'T GIVE US A CLOSE-UP OF THE TROLL NONONONO.
"What's his name?"

"He's name's none 'o your business."
"Hmm. That's a strange name."

Racefail of the Day: The circus master has a black strongman do his dirty work. Wearing a leopard skin. Wow, guys.

"You'll stay in the background until I arrive, is that clear?" Brig, rule 1 of companions: they never willingly "stay in the background."

Speaking of backgrounds, couldn't they just use some sort of wallpaper for the trees outside the phone booth? INSTEAD OF GREENSCREEN?

AND FOR THE KITCHEN? YOU SERIOUSLY DIDN'T HAVE A KITCHEN SET SOMEWHERE AT THE BBC?

Sorry I'm getting so irrationally mad about this, it's just...getting a little exasperating.

JO GRANT SMASH!

Three and Jo appear to be under siege by a circus lynch mob. Can't say I was expecting this.

OR THAT HOLY CRAP GET THEM OUT OF THERE.

and now they're in a fake police car probably driven by Autons and the Brig is in hot pursuit and omg

"It's some sort of a quarry." Well, at least they're going into familiar territory.

GHHHHHHHAAAAAAAAAAAAAAAAAFHKSDHAFKLDSHFKLD-SHFKL THAT FACE WHAT THE FLYING FUCK

DOCTOR SMASH! And, say it with me, RUN AWAY!

Jo blends into the foliage pretty well, but I'm a bit surprised Three's black cape and smoking jacket don't catch the enemy's eyes.

These are Yates' Determined Teeth.

"They're Autons! Bullets can't stop them!" I can tell the Brig is probably making an exasperated face on the inside.
Wait PLEASE TELL ME YATES IS GOING TO TRY AND RUN ONE OVER WITH THE CAR.

Firstly, YES. Secondly, wow, that was some impressive stunt work.

Meanwhile, back at the Mastercave...

"The more he struggles to postpone the moment, the greater the ultimate satisfaction." #notfreudianatall

"Now where was I..."
"Ten, sir."
("Three, sir!")

You know what I just realized Three and the Brig are like? Long-distance school friends who don't have problems until they move in together.

"You know, Jo, I sometimes think that 'military intelligence' is a contradiction in terms." Posting for classic-ness.

I think that's the first time the entire room's shaken when the TARDIS tries to take off. Also, billowing white smoke can't be a good sign.

"Doctor, stop being childish."
"What's wrong with being childish? I like being childish."
Somehow, Tom carries that a lot better than Jon.

Ohhhhhhhhh snap, that's the suffocating daffodil, isn't it?

WAIT A SECOND WHY WOULD ANYONE TAKE A FLOWER FROM SOMEONE WEARING A GIANT CARTOON HEAD SERIOUSLY WHAT'S WRONG WITH YOU PEOPLE

Oh god there's an army of them what the balls.

HANG ON. SINCE WHEN CAN THE AUTONS TALK. AND WHY DO THEY KINDA SOUND LIKE DALEKS.

Awww, Three's sticking up for the Brig. Although that's probably because this new guy called Three "some stray buffoon."

The evil plastics have started killing people in their homes. This...this is actually more disturbing than the majority of Classic monsters.
You know, with UNIT doing all that extensive research into the plastics companies, you'd like a name like "Masters" would've rung a bell.

Wait...why would the widow even keep the doll after all that? Oh right... #theplot *insert Operation joke here*

Ah HA! I KNEW the telephone guy looked suspicious...

Awww, Yates is making hot cocoa for Jo...with Three's Bunsen burner...right next to the heat-activated death doll...

JO JO TURN AROUND JO TURN AROUND JO JO JO TURN AROUND

Shoot a tiny Auton with one hand, hold two mugs and a can of cocoa in the other. Mike Yates, ladies and gentlemen.

So apparently the Master just keeps a live Auton in a safe....Sure, why not?

I bet I know what that phone cord's about to do...

Yup. And this is a Jon Pertwee's Face Appreciation Post.

"Help, Brigadier, HELP!" Probably the most satisfying thing the Brig's heard all serial, subconsciously speaking.

An hour and a half to stop the RAF from blowing a quarry all to shit? Three says: CHALLENGE ACCEPTED.

Maybe it's because I already know what the daffodils do, but part of me is looking at Three doing science and screaming "GET ON WITH IT."

HOLY CRAP. I thought the daffodils latched themselves onto people's faces, not shoot liquid plastic at them.

Suddenly, MASTER.

I love how general Classic attitude of Doctor and Master always tends to be some variant of "s'up, bro."

...Ah. Jo, I don't think you should've said that.

Well, at least Three still has a plan. And we've only got about 7-8 minutes left, so it's pretty sure to work.

Wow. That was pretty fast for getting out such a long message.

"Jo, it's a pity escapology wasn't part of your curriculum."
"Funny you should say that: look."
FREE HANDS!

Oh hey, Rex was alive this whole time! Although I can't expect that to last much longer...

What's that, Jo? You've hurt your ankle? Congratulations, you're a companion.

Looks like the Master's finally reached the point of "screw this, I'm finishing the job myself."

So they've got...3-4 minutes to resolve everything. That might be just a tad tricky.

"Change the polarity!" And...that seems to magically fix everything. Okay, cool.

The Master seems to be surrendering, which is Masterspeak for "I've got a cunning plan up my sleeve."

But then he got shot repeatedly and...OHHHHHH WAIT, I SEE WHAT YOU DID THERE.

Oh. Actually, I was partly right, but I wasn't expecting THAT. Poor Rex. His mother loses a husband and a son in one serial.

"Think he'll turn up again, Doctor?"
"Mmm, bound to."
"You don't seem very worried about it."
"I'm not. As a matter of fact, Jo, I'm rather looking forward to it."
Get used to it, Doctor. He'll be around even through your tenth incarnation.

Originally Posted October 21st, 2011

THE MIND OF EVIL

Written by Don Houghton
Aired: January 30 – March 6, 1971

Ah yes, this one still needs to be colored in, doesn't it?

(Yeah, when I said I'd finished the entire black and white era of Doctor Who, I'd completely forgotten about these stories.)

"That looks like Dracula's castle!" I wonder if they're in Whitby...

Aww, Three's so happy waving to the camera and then the mean ol' security man comes and stops him.

Okay, they're not in Whitby, they're in the LOUDEST PRISON EVER.

So Three and Jo traveled out here to watch a man being executed out of "scientific curiosity." #familyentertainment

Ohhhhhh I get it, it's not an execution, it's Science.

A machine that extracts "evil impulses" from the human brain? Funny, I was just reading Dr. Jekyll and Mr. Hyde earlier tonight...

So that one dude basically just announced that he has a box full of evil sitting around. GEE, I DON'T SEE THIS GOING WRONG AT ALL.

Actually, things went wrong a lot faster than I thought they were going to.

Fffffftttttt that other guy's face is pretty priceless right now. Carried out satisfactorily indeed.

Ho boy, the Brig's not going to be happy when Three dumps even more work on his plate.

Chin Lee! I've heard of you! I think this is the first time we've had an Asian character in Who since the monks in The Abominable Snowmen.

And she starts by offending the Brig. This probably won't go down well.

OR SHE COULD MANAGE TO SILENCE THE BRIG WITH THE POWER OF GLARES. I LIKE THIS WOMAN VERY MUCH ALREADY.

And then she blames the theft on "those imperialist Americans." Hey, we weren't THAT bad in the 70's, were we? Oh wait... #vietnam

Aww, childrens. But wait...why is she setting something on fire near a playground?

Answer: because that somewhat conspicuous mind-control probe told her to. Of course, people don't usually look behind other people's ears.

Meanwhile back at Science Prison...there goes another slip of "is the Doctor several thousand years old?"

Wait wait wait WHO goes around accusing the Doctor of not being scientist?!?

"We've got real trouble this time, the Chinese delegate's dead!" Wow. The Brig sure knows how to end a scene.

Well, now we know: when you leave a box full of evil lying around, it will eventually become sentient and start killing people.

Okay, so it's not a box. Actually, it's a more literal version of how TV Tropes would probably put it: Sealed Evil in a Can. Or canister.

So it's pretty clear that the Box of Evil makes people die from their worst fear but...how exactly does it cause the physical evidence?

Uh oh, the evidence seems to be pointing towards mind-controlled Chin Lee being the murderer. And the Brig is catching on. To a degree.

AND she may have been the assistant for installing the Box of Evil. Welp. Can't say I was expecting that.

I only just realized: thank you, Jo, for having the sense to wear pants instead of mini-skirts all the time.

Yes, I know she wears mini-skirts in some stories, but this is not one of them.

Suddenly FIRE.

Jo Grant to the rescue! Aww, she gets to return the favor from her mind-screwing in the last story.

You know, Three, you could...like...I dunno...thank her, or something.

New Who tends to shy away from revealing the darkest corners of the Doctor's mind, but this one is being nice and giving us some outright.

To clarify: we never saw what was in his room in The God Complex, but here they're referring back to Inferno as the source of his fear.

Umm, Yates, rule of thumb: NEVER threaten to use force on Three. He WILL out-badass you.

Doctor, when will you learn that telling your companions to stay put and do as they're told only works about 10% of the time?

Meanwhile, Benton Coat Porn.

And now he's being attacked by the Box of Evil at long-distance through Chin Lee. I wonder what he's afraid of...

Oh, I guess we won't get to see it. Oh well.

Uh oh, Benton's got some s'plainin' to do to the Brig. And Brig is not happy.

"You're too delicate for intelligence work, Benton, you'd better go lie down." Too delicate. *Too delicate.* #toodelicate

The Brig is actually much more frightening and much less amusing when he's legitimately angry than when he's just annoyed.

Outside, the Master finally reveals himself. It was in-tents.

Funny thing is, that rubber disguise mask he was using doesn't look that different from his real face.

Awwww, all it takes to turn Three from a tiger to a kitten is assure him that you'll blow up that evil box he hates.

"Cheshire cat, Yates, Cheshire cat." UNIT IS A PACK OF KITTIES.

Cool, we get the Doctor speaking Chinese with subtitles!

"It is rare to meet a Westerner who knows my language." A little attention to culture goes a long way. #importantlifelessonsfromDoctorWho

Hang on, that wasn't Chinese, that was Hokkien. Never heard of that language before... #themoreyouknow

Now that Mao has come into the picture ever so slightly, I'm starting to see more blatant connections to the Red Scare in this story.

(Although I honestly don't know if the Red Scare was as big a deal in the UK as it was in the US.)

Miffed Brig is miffed. And when the Brig is miffed, he SHOOTS... em, SITS on something!

Aww, Jo's being so nice and sweet to the ex-con who got his mind scrambled. I guess they'd both have something to talk about...

The jail janitor just planted a gun under the pillow. Somehow I don't see this ending well.

This scene is giving me a tiny craving for tea. I'd gladly oblige myself if I had anything decaffeinated on hand.

Meanwhile, Brig...never change. Ever.

Also, this man REALLY doesn't like you. Trying repeatedly to talk to him might not be such a good idea.

Unexpected Introduction of Nuclear Warhead. I wonder where this plot could possibly be headed...

Delgado with a cigar. This episode just became about 5x classier.

Hello, Token American Guy! Accent's not too shabby.

Chinese trying to kill Americans in the 70's. Subtle, guys. Really subtle.

And the American even sees her as a dragon. ...Why.

So hopefully the fact that the American's attempted death scene happened as a cliffhanger is an implication that he gets saved. Let's see...

I was right, but HOLY CRAP CHIN LEE IS AN *ACTUAL* DRAGON?

"A collective hallucination, gentlemen, nothing more." That was my second guess. Thank you, Three.

Question of the evening: are all the Chinese dialects just the writer showing off or did they actually have to do serious research for this?

"If you've got any sense, you'll get some beddy-byes. Good night." Sound advice for half the people online ever. #gpoy

Cut from Benton yelling and being assertive to the Brig sleeping at his desk. Awwwwwww...

"It's Yates. He's had a hold-up with his...erm...cargo."
"Yes, well tell him to be careful with his, erm, cargo."

"Cargo" is now an innuendo. Thank you, gentlemen.

Displeased Master is displeased.

I just realized, Nicholas Courtney could've given quite the masterclass on telephone acting. So many reaction shots per episode.

And then Jo Grant graced the crisis with a touch of her badassery. Even as Delgado, the Master liked to carry his own soundtrack around with him. #likeaboss

Wait, does the guy welcoming the Master right now look remarkably like Richard Nixon to anyone else?

Yikes, every gun in this prison seems to be loaded with Instant Kill Bullets.

Huh. Looks like Delgado's prowess at speaking through gas masks was wildly superior to Simm's.

Good ol' Three, brushing aside guns in your face is one thing, but only great men can brush aside rifles.

Oh Delgado!Master, you're such a Bond villain. Now if only I'd seen some actual '60s Bond to compare you to...

"Oh, it won't harm me. I created it!" On the other hand, you don't seem to be Genre Savvy enough to know just how wrong you are right now.

Hello again, Nuclear Missile Plot Device! I almost missed you, except I didn't.

Roger Delgado, you have quite possibly one of the shiniest foreheads I've ever seen on Doctor Who.

And once again the Doctor is saved by: a glass of water!

Close-ups of Jon Pertwee's starey-eyes will never not be some level of really creepy.

There's a "you...me...and handcuffs" joke staring me so hard in the face it's practically plucking my eyebrows.

Three does not look particularly happy about the Master feeling him up like that.

On the other hand, he IS Genre Savvy enough to challenge the Master on his hook-me-up-to-an-evil-machine-and-then-leave-the-room tactic.

Well Master, looks like your little scheme didn't go as planned after all. That's what you get for saying "I made it, so it's perfect, etc." Awww, and now he's playing doctor to the Doctor.

Wow. I don't think I've seen Three in this bad a state since Inferno. Also he's got sweat EVERYWHERE.

Well at least he's reunited with Jo now, that ought to help things along.

So, whenever you guys hear someone say that the Doctor "needs a doctor," does that mar the drama of the scene at all? Or is that just me?

Huh. So it looks like the Box of Evil wasn't gaining sentience, it was sentient from the beginning. Can't say I was expecting that.

And the little bugger seems to be overpowering the Master. His greatest fear? Terrifying Pertwee.

(For the record, Jon Pertwee's Evil Laugh is pretty intense in its own right. I don't blame the Master for being freaked out by it.)

Jo Grant, you have entirely too many rings on your hand. #the70s

I just realized: Three is the first Doctor to only have one companion at a time, excluding the UNIT chaps, so he has a much more direct responsibility to his companions as a mentor figure, particularly with Jo.

Although, I'm honestly not sure if he counted much as a mentor figure to Liz, since she was already rather independent from the start.

Master says, time for a slideshow from my evil plans! I mean...vacation!

Jo Grant wants FOOD, dammit!

Now THAT'S what I call a food fight. #forgivethepun #imsorry

Huh. Considering Three seems to know what the Master's plan is, he's being remarkably cool and calm about it.

Suddenly, AMBUSH. And Yates goes skidding away, complete with cartoon sound effects.

Just a rule of thumb for next time: please don't leave Benton for dead. He'll be fine for quite a while yet.

For some reason, I feel like there's an obvious joke to be made about Yates riding a motorcycle, but I honestly have no idea why.

Yates is captured, Benton's patched up, and srys Three is srys. Looks like the missile plot is overtaking the Box of Evil plot here. Or maybe they're running side by side now.

Woah. Apparently the Box has teleportation powers. Or something.

Aww, baby's first steps. Of DEATH.

So I take it every single cliffhanger in this story is going to involve someone being attacked by the Box? Only one more to find out.

Aww, I love how the reformed ex-con is such an innocent docile creature now. He hears loud scary noises and goes looking for his Jo.

(Seriously, if something bad happens to him between now and the end, I will be a sad panda.)

Huh. I think that's the first UNIT officer I've seen with glasses on. Pretty big ones, too.

Yikes. I've never seen any human get under the Master's skin quite like Mailer is here. Seriously, that's frighteningly impressive.

Yates seems rather calm and collected about the prospect of being held as a hostage. "It did cross my mind..."

Master, Three and Jo aren't interested in your plans to blow the world to crap, can't you see they're playing checkers?

Looks like Benton's being temporarily replaced by Major Glasses while his head gets better. Still, I like this new guy.

Oh wait, never mind, Benton walked in literally right after I typed that.

"Benton you're supposed to be suffering from severe concussion!" The way he says that almost sounds like "Benton, why aren't you suffering?"

Meanwhile in the Mastercave, Yates escapes! Except not really.

Except yes really! Mike SMASH.

Okay. The Master is being Three's lab assistant to literally help him lasso the Box of Evil before it runs away. This show, you guys.

Aaaaand now the lasso's catching fire. This may or may not end well.

Hey Mailer, somehow I don't think scratching your nose with a gun barrel is really the best idea. (But in your case, go ahead.)

Awww, I love how Jo gets to be so motherly towards Three here. I love any companion who gets to look after the Doctor like that.

Three was once in the Tower of London with Sir Walter Raleigh after a dispute with Elizabeth I about potatoes? So many Blackadder jokes...

Cockney-Brig. This is happening, you guys. COCKNEY-BRIG.

Hey guy on the roof, general rule of thumb: do NOT shoot the megaphone out of the Brig's hands when he's talking. He doesn't like that.

Okay, so I guess not every cliffhanger involved the Box screwing with somebody, but MAILER YOU JUST SHOT THE DOCTOR.

And of course the shot missed because BRIG TO THE RESCUE!

"Thank you, Brigadier, but do you think for once in your life you could arrive BEFORE the nick of time?"
"It's nice to see you too, Doctor."

Wow. The Brig almost never looks sheepish, but sweet holy hell he looks downright dumbstruck-by-his-own-fail in this shot.

More importantly, Yates to the rescue! Beginning of the last episode and we know where to find our main villain/weapon...

"No need to worry about the Master anymore, this time we've got him." Ohhhhhhhhhh you say that NOW but just. you. wait.

Pffffffftt. It's kind of hilarious how you can tell that they achieved this shot by just waving the camera violently around. Very violently.

Wait. NO. BENTON. YOU DID NOT JUST SET IN MOTION THE SERIES OF EVENTS THAT I THINK YOU DID.

Oh. Hang on, never mind, that actually might be doing more good than harm.

To clarify: it looks like the brainwashed guy's newfound innocence is taming the Box of Evil instead of the Box killing him.

And now we finally get to see into the Box to behold the creature within: it kinda looks like Scaroth's liquified head.

"Acting Governor Sergeant Benton here."
"...Who?"
I almost want to say that there's a prank-calling-UNIT joke in here somewhere.

Dr. Summers comes in, doesn't listen to Jo, and things, as they apparently say in the UK, look about to go tits up.

Or maybe not. On the other hand, Three, somehow I don't think the Master will want to leave now that he knows you're here.

So the brainwashed ex-con's name is Barnham. Only took me nearly the entire serial to figure that out.

The Master's air-car-driving-hands will never not be hilarious.

Wait. NO. NO BARNHAM. DON'T STOP TO HELP THE MASTER. HE'S THE BAD GUY. BAD. GUY.

And now he's gone and run you over with a fucking van. And now you're *dead.* Not cool, guys. Just...not cool.

Three, I'm sorry to be such a Debbie Downer but...this is the Master we're talking about. Of COURSE he has the circuit.

Also, "not for quite some time" means "until the next serial."

Aww, Brig looks so happy to have Three stuck on Earth with him.

Originally Posted November 24th, 2011

THE CLAWS OF AXOS

Written by Bob Baker and Dave Martin
Aired: March 13 – April 3, 1971

GHHHHAHHH. Hello giant space slug with Flailing Spaghetti Monster inside please go away and leave us alone. (Seriously that ship is gross.)

I'm waaaay more impressed with the way the Brig leans on that file cabinet than I really have any right to.

"What about this Doctor? I gather he's not a British subject, but then WHO is he and WHERE does he come from?!?" That door, apparently.

Wait a second who's this American guy trying to be Errol Flynn for Jo. That...made no sense.

I can only assume Three's cabin fever is the cause of his hissy fits and current wardrobe choice (shiny purple on maroon velvet? Really?)

Errol Flynn Guy standing up to Angry Glasses Guy is actually doing a halfway decent job of getting me to ignore the former's iffy accent.

And that mysterious rapid-fire noise in the background was coming from...where?

Hang on, mysterious tramp spluttering around on a bicycle...PIGBIN JOSH! We meet at last.

"Shoot first and think afterwards, is that it?" I was wondering when Three was going to say something like that.

Woah. I think there's a bit of a difference between "sudden snowstorms" and INSTANT SNOW EVERYWHERE.

Okay...does Pigbin Josh's theme sound a little like The Itsy Bitsy Spider to anyone else?

Yikes. Falling headlong into a pond in the middle of winter? Forget instant snow, this calls for instant pneumonia.

You know what, I'm just going to come out and say it: that ship is way too vaginal and probably scarred a lot of boys for life. #wtfhannah

Ah yes, and here goes Three into his "I'm just going to stand here talking and be better than you" mode.

"Jo...I'm sorry, not this time." On the contrary, Three, yes EVERY time.

Oh. Well maybe that wasn't Pigbin Josh if his face just...collapsed in on itself...ew...

Wow. Say what you want about Classic Who's budget problems, but for some reason I REALLY love that random eye in the wall.

That awkward moment when the InfoText of a Jon Pertwee serial solves the mystery of a J-Lo lyric that you couldn't quite make out.

Wait a sec, there's about a dozen UNIT soldiers surrounding Axos and yet Jo STILL got inside with no resistance at all? ...Well okay then.

Ah, hello Master, I was wondering where you'd got off to.

("This is, says the script, 'the ad-man's dream Coca-Cola family.'") OR IT COULD BE DUDES IN LATEX AND GOLD HEADS. HOW DOES THAT MAKE SENSE.

Ah. That's how it makes sense.

Well, the Axons seem harmless enough, although Three's catching their plotholes like flies which seems to imply The Contrary.

Awwww, froggie!

"This is, I presume, one of your food animals." Actually, it's a toad. #mybad #andyourstoo

Jo, I must admit, that's the most strangled-sounding scream I've ever heard from a companion in a cliffhanger.

The Axons are calling Jo on hallucination. I think I know exactly where this is going.

Also, I can't tell if the Axons are supposed to be wearing skin suits or if that's just shoddy costuming.

Somehow I think Jo's retort would've worked better if the autofocus had gotten its act together faster.

"That ganglion on the wall behind you - see it?" Oh, you mean that bundle of garden hose? Yeah, I see it.

Not sure how it took me so long to realize that Mr. Chinn was probably named such because of that gigantic second chin. Seriously.

I'm also becoming increasingly convinced that he represents some sort of political allegory, but I can't think of any events to link it to.

In any other circumstance I'd be pretty iffy about the Brig pointing a gun at a government official, but...this situation calls for it.

On a completely unrelated note, glad to see Three's back in something more stylish. I love red and white on black.

On the other hand, it would be a little nice if he'd focus more on the all-of-UNIT-just-got-arrested thing and less on the Axonite mystery.

Speaking of which, ALL OF UNIT JUST GOT ARRESTED.

Poor Pigbin Josh, all crumbled away (turns out that was him, since he was named in the credits.)

The scientist in the brown coat seems to know something about FTL travel, since his lightspeed meter goes about 4x past the speed of light.

Cue Three going into "aww, you little humans are trying to discover time travel, that's so cute" mode.

Apparently one of this story's working titles was "The Vampire From Space." (Or, State of Decay, if you will.)

I keep hearing from fandom that the Axons are a vampiric race, but I haven't really seen any evidence of that so far...

So according to the InfoText, the real naughty symbols I should be seeing in this serial are the eyestalks. (Thank you, crew.)

He's climbin' out your Axos, 'n shootin' your soldiers up... #hideyourdoctors #hideyourjos #coshaszappinerrebodyouthere

And Files makes a last-second escape! Let's hope he survives long enough to find Jo again.

Meanwhile, the Master is now James Bond.

Whoops, it's not "Files," it's "Filer." And I have an unfortunate feeling that it's the fake one that just found Three.

"OUT OF THE WAY, DOC!" AND THEN HE GOT HIS ACTUAL ERROL FLYNN MOMENT. Although it must be pretty freaky, shooting your other self.

Well, that made quick work of fake!Filer. Quick...bubbly work.

Put the Axonite in the particle accelerator because it's time to DO SCIENCE TO IT! Also, the dial goes up to 6x the speed of light. Wow.

Oh don't mind the guy on the floor, he's just trying to get out of that sheet. Those giant tentacle monsters, on the other hand...

On a completely unrelated note, I love that "Action by Havoc" is an actual credit on this show.

So, again, can we just call these things Walking Spaghetti Monsters? Filer has been touched by their noodley appendage.

Oh wait, never mind, they're the Axons wearing...big...red...noodle suits. ...Well okay then.

Put that gun away, can't you see the Brig's on the phone?

I would make an "I've seen enough hentai to know where this is going" joke, but I'm not going to. (Besides, it just writes itself.)

So, why exactly are the Axons communicating with Three and Jo through a '70s music video?

Actually I can still see the Axon's original image as a perfectly decent concept for benevolent aliens. Shame they had to have rotten cores.

Oh cool, the Ministry of Defense has Skype!

Poor Filer, trying to yell plot details in his sleep...

GEE, I SURE HOPE THAT MYSTERIOUS UNIT OFFICIAL WITH HIS FACE HIDDEN ISN'T THE MASTER BECAUSE *THAT* WOULD BE *BAD.*

WELL GOLLY GEE WILIKERS BATMAN, IT IS THE MASTER!

And then everyone had a fuchsia seizure.

And then everyone had a green seizure.

Sorry Canada, you only get one unit of Axonite.

Have fun with the Axonite kthxbai.

I'm sorry Filer, I love you but your accent is...really...really...not holding up very well.

You know you're the Brig when a simple walk to an office is interrupted by wait-a-sec-why-does-that-man-have-golden-tentacles-on-his-head.

I'm seeing the spaghetti Axon walking across that bridge and all I can think is "I MUST SLOW-JOG BACK TO MY PEOPLE!"

"I will shoot at him!" said the UNIT grunt who WAS THEN EXPLODED IN A BIG BALL OF FIRE OH MY GOD.

Alrighty, the Brig has his Benton and his Yates, time to kick some Axon tail...er...tentacle.

"It's like trying to fly a second-hand gas stove!" Hey Master, I'll save you the trouble: this will not work.

Also, you appear to be color-blind as well because you seem to have not noticed the trio of green figures that have now surrounded you.

I'm honestly wondering if Yates' current pose has any actual strategic value or if he's just like that to look badass.

And then the Master tossed him his laser gun so Benton can cuff him. This day is looking up for UNIT!

On the other hand, the Master just had an excellent opportunity to test his grand-scale hostage plan for Logopolis, and he took it.

(Okay, so he wasn't holding the universe hostage, but everyone's got to start somewhere.)

Roger Delgado, I really like your face.

Three makes his escape! Although I have to admit, that's a pretty comfy-looking hostage chair.

And the male fandom rejoiced at a full four seconds of Jo Grant's knickers.

Wow. I think that's the first time in the show that the Doctor has ever hit one of his companions, even as a snap-out-of-it gesture.

I know they've said that regeneration is supposed to feel like a bad LSD trip, but this sequence doesn't seem to far off either. #the70s

"My dear Brigadier, I promised to help you, not sort out ALL your problems!" Not if the Brig has anything to say about it...

I love how the earlier Master's presence could feel a lot more casual than Simm. Like here he's just chilling on the railing with the Brig.

Wait...okay, I think the only way Hardiman could've gone off the railing like that is if he'd somersaulted backwards on a trampoline.

Hah, Master tries to make his escape but then Three's like "s'up?" and the Master's like "okay fine geez."

And now it's time for UNIT Home Movies, with Mike Yates. Today's episode: Filming Vampiric Monstrosities From Space.

The piercing look of "HAH, I WIN" the Brig is throwing at Chinn in this scene is excellent. The chicken leg just makes everything better.

So of COURSE it isn't until Filer says he's from the NYPD that he starts to sound a little like a New Yorker.

Yikes. I honestly can't tell if Three is just bluffing to butter the Master up or if he's actually that desperate to leave Earth.

Somehow, I don't think dematerialization theory will be enough to get you off Earth. I think you need ACTUAL knowledge of dematerialization.

Huh. Looks like if you went through those doors, you'd walk right into a Troughton serial. SEE IF IT'S ONE OF THE LOST EPISODES.

Benton and Yates vs. Spaghetti Axons. Round One FIGHT!

UNIT Chaps WIN. FIREBALL-TALITY.

...oh snap, Three's actually serious about leaving. "Goodbye, Jo. I shall miss you."

Waaaaaaaaaaait a sec...now we finally come to The Reveal.

That...doesn't seem to make things much better, actually. We've got about 8 minutes to wrap everything up...

Ah, now THAT'S more like it: when in doubt, throw it into a time loop.

Looks like the besieged UNIT folks are going to be just fine after all, thanks to the Spaghetti Axons conveniently vanishing into thin air.

Axons, humping the Doctor isn't going to solve your problems either.

On the other hand, Three hiding from a particle-accelerator-induced explosion in the TARDIS will probably keep him from getting blown up.

Sure guys, run back to the wreckage of a power plant RIGHT after it explodes. I'm sure that's not dangerous at ALL.

"Well it's perfectly simple, Brigadier: a time loop is its...erm...well it's ermweirew...it's a time loop!"

Actually, I think the real question here is, why are you having this conversation in a burned-out office? Couldn't you go somewhere... safer?

Or at least nicer? And...you know...not missing an entire wall?

"It seems that I'm some kind of a galactic yo-yo!" Have fun with that, Three. We'll just sit here and watch you spin your hands around.

Originally Posted December 31st, 2011

COLONY IN SPACE

Written by Malcolm Hulke
Aired: April 10 – May 15, 1971

Wow. I never thought I'd say this in Doctor Who but...my brain is listening for the Star Trek TOS opening sequence here.

Hello Time Lords, up to your manipulative douchebaggery again?

Also, the criminal photo of the Doctor on the screen further confirms my theory that Gallifreyan writing is different every time we see it.

"One of my agents thinks he's picked up traces of the Master."
"Your agents are ALWAYS picking up traces of the Master."

Aww, well at least Three and Jo can still giggle about UNIT arresting important political figures by accident.

"Well, what've you got in there anyway, policemen?"
"Why not step inside and see for yourself?"
So Jo's only just now getting in the TARDIS.

Yes, I know that Liz Shaw never got to go inside, but that's a different story.

"I don't believe it! It's bigger inside than out!" It's...also still got the Troughton walls.

Actually, is it just me, or is Pertwee's console room a little different in every pre-Three Doctors story?

Brig. *Brig.* Can I just take you and your gloriously nonchalant reactions to the Doctor doing things and keep you in my pocket forever.

Like Gallifreyan writing, the Time Vortex looks a bit different every time, too. This time it's yet another 70's music video.

It's kind of adorably sad how Jo has the most doe-eyed please-take-me-home-now-Doctor reaction of any of the accidental-takeoff companions.

Also, hello Upgraded War Machine, what might you be doing here with that grappling crane arm?

Wait, that's not a grappling crane at all, that's a...giant metal detector? Well it's certainly a giant something-detector.

"Is that supposed to be where we are?" I can just hear Patsy from Monty Python in the background going "It's just a model."

After UNIT, it's really fascinating seeing how sudden space-and-time travel is adding a whole new dimension to Three and Jo's relationship.

In a weird way, it's like watching Hartnell again. Namely that the companions are so torn between fear, disbelief, and fascination.

(I say Hartnell instead of Troughton because most of Two's companions chose to come along for the ride.)

(Also, and more importantly, Jo's reaction feels strangely reminiscent of Ian and Barbara's first few experiences in the TARDIS.)

(The major difference here is, of course, the fact that Jo and Three have already built up a relationship and she knows she can trust him.)

"Come on, Jo, nothing to worry about." Yeah, don't worry, the Doctor's had plenty of experience with quarries.

Eugh, and these must be the native species. Nice shiny things, though.

Well, it's good to know that the Doctor's desire for exploration has gone down from "let's go see that Dalek city" to "oh hey a rock."

(I mean this purely in terms of likelihood of companion endangerment, of course.) Oh hello Random Dude With a Gun.

I have to admit, it's rather striking just how Earth-like this space colony is. Framed photos and books and everything.

Actually, with the leather-like outfits and facial hair all over the place, it almost looks post-medieval.

OH NOES, NOT MINERALOGISTS. WHAT COULD POSSIBLY BE WORSE THAN A MINERALOGIST.

Somehow I doubt the Time Lords sent Three to this world to help them with farming trouble. Cue obligatory Someone Dragging the TARDIS Off.

Forget what I said about "medieval": with crop failures and that girl's dress, this is turning into Little House on the Prairie in Space.

Ohhhhhhh the year was 2471, HOW I WISH I WAS IN SHERBROOKE NOOOWWWWWWWW... #obscurecamppreferences

Alrighty, now THIS is starting to look more like the future in space.

Suddenly GIANT IGUANA.

Wow. Usually it's some random mook who's the first to die, but this time it's a happy married couple. That's...frighteningly grim.

So there's not only another colony that's been destroyed but the creepy things with spears also might not be dangerous? Welp.

Considering the robot that just burst in has the letters MC on it I'll bet it's one of those mining machines they were talking about before.

Huh. I just realized that they're still calling them "episodes" and not "parts."

Also, that was probably one of the most anti-climactic cliffhanger follow-ups I've seen in a while.

"Interplanetary Mining Corporation." I KNEW IT.

"The usual story, that we've only just arrived and we're surprised and shocked that the place has been colonized." I DIDN'T KNEW IT.

"Make yourself at home. That's the entertainment console." But what would Three want with "entertainment" when there's Science in the room?

Especially when the "entertainment" is just fear-mongering war footage?

So it sounds like these guys disguise themselves as giant killer lizards to scare off colonists. ...What kind of mining company IS this?!?

Also they say things like this: "Look at this report. LOOK AT IT!!!" #IWANTALLOFYOUTOLOOKATIT

Seems Three has had enough of watching propaganda and has drawn the Bullshit Curtain.

I find it an interesting coincidence that the IMC's uniform is the same black-and-red scheme as Three's outfit in this serial.

Also I just noticed that this is a fairly companion-lite episode so far. We're nearly halfway done and Jo's only had one scene.

In the meantime, TIME-FU.

There's a "get in, loser, we're going ass kicking" joke I should make with Three one of these days, best to make note of it now.

Meanwhile, back at the Little House on the Prairie in Space, Jo Grant's in the kitchens. Well then.

Okay, this has to be said: design-wise, these are some of the worst aliens I've seen in Doctor Who. They really are.

"Don't worry, Jim'll fix it." Jo's giggle makes me wonder if that show was around when this story aired...

...huh. According to Wikipedia it was still a few years off. But if we take UNIT dating into accordance...MALCOLM HULKE CAN TELL THE FUTURE.

In the meantime, that straggler you guys picked up has just lost it again and killed your only electrician. Nice going.

Waaaaaaaaaait. Either that guy is *actually* inside or he's really an insider for the IMC. The latter is suddenly looking more likely.

Okay, why do they feel the need to zoom in on the mining ship's number every time they cut back there?

Welp. We seem to be in almost exactly the same cliffhanger as the last episode.

Another catastrophe averted by Time-Fu. Also, those giant claw arms on the robot are becoming increasingly hilarious.

So the mining corps and the colonists finally meet. The former aren't making a terribly good first impression.

They're talking about adjudicators and suddenly all I can think about are Chris and Roz from the New Adventures. Same group?

"Doctor! You haven't lost the TARDIS?"
"Well no, I haven't exactly 'lost' it, let's say it's 'temporarily mislaid'."

Wait, since when does this corporation have a piece of the Key to Time? Also, looks like I was right about the refugee working for them.

Wow, Jo sure didn't have a problem getting onto their ship. Although I don't like the looks of those bulkhead doors...

I'm sorry guys but I hear the IMC's leader's name is Captain Dent and suddenly I'm seeing Arthur Dent and aagggggghhh fandom scramble.

Holding Jo hostage and then chaining her to explosives just so they can eventually mine the planet clean. Jeez, these people are DICKS.

And Jo is being delightfully nonchalant about this. That's our lil' escapologist!

"Well, I took a class in escapology...once..." Aaaaaand thank you for ruining the magic.

Also, this is looking like another case of Selflessness Will Get You Caught.

Huh. Someone correct me if I'm wrong, but I think this is the first time we've had a space story where the guns had bullets and not lasers.

I would make a "we'll befriend you with our SPACE GUNS!" joke here but there are no crowbars and nobody would get the reference.

"Don't bother, I got him for you!" DDDD:

I would say this means Jo's sacrifice is in vain, but now we've got a guy riddled with the IMC's bullet holes. Evidence!

OR NOT. Looks like the IMC have a dissenter in their midst as well!

"I'm not one of Dent's killers, I'm a miner." FINALLY, someone who's actually there to do their job.

Ah, so he wants the colonists off the planet too, but at least it's for let's-not-spill-anymore-blood reasons.

Meanwhile, good ol' fashioned Tape In Space!

So it looks like Jo might be on the road to safety when Suddenly Aliens.

Violence and innocent-looking girls solve everything. #itarefact

Well it looks like the colonists got the upper hand on the miners pretty quickly, but we're only halfway through the serial, so...

Next Phase: getting Jo out of Iraq. I mean, a rock.

That was an unforgivable pun and I apologize.

So...are the primitives supposed to look like they're splattered with blood, or is that a design quirk?

Awwww, lookit the giant iguana!

(But seriously, how they got the machine with claws and that handheld projector to fool anyone is beyond me.)

The adjudicator's finally here, but somehow I doubt that's going to make things much better at this point.

I guess that's the leader of the primitives. From the big flowing cape I thought he might be the Master (seriously, where IS he this time?)

Everyone on the IMC ship seems to be in a state of Everything Could Go Wrong If One Person Does Something Reckless Or Stupid.

Aaaaaand there we go, secret gun in the drawer. Crap. Then again, as everyone's been saying, "how will THIS look to the adjudicator?"

Three looks like he's going for a leisurely stroll, not rushing to rescue his companion.

Waaaaiiiit, hold up, is the adjudicator...?

...THERE'S the Master! I was wondering where you'd got to! (On the other hand, everyone is now screwed.)

On that note, the fact that the primitives are gesturing towards the picture of what Three thought was a sacrifice doesn't bode well either.

I think this is the first time I've seen people give an honest attempt at diplomatic resolution on this show instead of shooting each other.

On the other hand, there was already a lot of shooting and that fact that the Master is the mediator renders all sense of fair trial moot.

Also there was quite a bit of diplomacy in Cold Blood, but that was much later.

So THAT'S where Jon Pertwee and His Magical Face Money came from!

Wait, if the primitives can read minds, then how did they fall for that trick?

More importantly, do Three and Jo know for absolute certain that the primitives are planning to sacrifice them?

AND HOW ARE THE PRIMITIVES NOT HEARING ALL THIS WHISPERING?

Well, that escape plan didn't work out too well, did it?

"All intruders in the city must die. That is the law." Well. That answers that question.

Whew. At least the leader is willing to listen to reason and let them go.

I don't think I've ever heard the word "overjoyed" spoken with such assertion before. Thank you, Three.

"Three different races or three mutations of the same race?" Now THAT'S an interesting theory.

Huh. Looks like the Master may've been trying to conduct actual diplomacy after all.

Especially since he's just continuing to announce the verdict even after Three and Jo burst in and find him.

Okay, so no verdict yet, but he sure is taking this opportunity to taunt Three about "lol I have my papers in order and you don't."

Verdict in favor of the miners (as expected), but at least he made it sound like a reasonable argument.

Well, enough of pseudo courtroom drama, let's get drunk!

I just realized something: all of time and space, and yet the Doctor almost never returns to the same planet twice.

I mean there's only so many conceivably habitable worlds out there, how many stories could be done by revisiting planets in the past/future?

I know this has been done with places like Skaro and Peladon, but I think it could be taken advantage of more often.

"The Master came to this planet for a purpose, Jo." EXACTLY WHAT I'VE BEEN WONDERING FOR A WHILE.

Seriously, I don't see anything the Master has to gain from this. He's already perfected forgery so he can get himself nearly anywhere.

Of course, forgery alone won't get your TARDIS working...

Naturally Norton is finally found out by just one guy who immediately gets shot. At least the communicator is out of commission now.

SHOOTOUT IN THE WAREHOUSE.

Master, with all due respect, this has to be one of the lamest plans to kill the Doctor you've ever had.

Wow, this serial really has an unfortunate tendency towards massively lame cliffhanger follow-ups.

Well, at least the colonists are in control again. Although I'm not sure how this makes them much better than the miners.

I still have absolutely no idea whose side the Master is supposed to be on or what he ultimately hopes to gain from this whole fiasco.

And that, my dear Three, was the sound of that credentials conversation from earlier coming back to bite you in the ass.

And while I appreciate your convenient possession of the Master's TARDIS key, don't you think he would've noticed it was missing by now?

Captain Dent is the first one to see reason and do a background check on the Master's adjudicator claim? Can't say I was expecting that.

Looks like the Master at least has some security measures in place on his TARDIS. A laser trip-wire seems a bit basic for him, though.

wiggle wiggle wiggle

Ticker tape! In Space!

Wait. No. Jo, please tell me you did not just actually do that. Those things work both ways.

Intruders in my TARDIS? Quick! Activate the poison gas and slow-moving disco lights!

Apparently when counting down to landing, you reach a point where you just stop using even numbers.

Okay, so it was knockout gas and not poison gas, but still.

IMC security personnel: they also double as ninjas.
Oh hey, even more shooting.

You can tell I've been on a bit of a Star Wars bent lately because I keep expecting Three to Force that stick out of the Master's hand.

Wait a sec, how does Dent have ruling power all of a sudden? And what was up with that key-dropping?

Dent is really good at dick moves. Withholding vital damming evidence so he can keep his power.

And now I know where that Evil Hugs picture came from.

Oh, never mind that our ride just got pummeled by giant falling rocks, I still own your ass.

Once again, Caldwell might be the colonists' only sliver of hope for survival from the IMC...

Ahhhhhhhhhh, THAT'S what the key-dropping was for!

Naturally the Master is not taking too kindly to this. #itoldyoubro #iwarnedyouaboutkeys

Okay, so Three didn't Force the rod out of the Master's hands, but he sure did kick it.

World-building question: is there really a need for the doors to be shaped like that? Looks rather counter-intuitive. #lightningboltdoors

And now, Anthropology Hour with Theta and Koschei.

Ahhhhhhhhhh, so THAT'S why the Target novel of this serial is called "Doctor Who and the Doomsday Weapon!"

FINALLY. Thank you, Master. Everything makes sense now. A really cheap sense, but sense.

Breathing device for potentially dangerous gas? Nah, Three's got a hankie.

"Then you can sit in your ship till you rot. Try to get out and you'll be shot on the spot." A bit too much...rhyming for something so dire?

So of course the first thing I notice about this fight scene is WOW that is some impressive mud.

I can only assume it rained pretty heavily at the quarry because seriously you guys, this mud.

Umm...if you're going to blow up a spaceship full of innocent people, you might want to make the poignant aftermath longer than 20 seconds.

ESPECIALLY if said innocent people are the underdogs we've been rooting for for the past 5 episodes. Seriously.

Well, Jo and Caldwell certainly got over that pretty quickly...

"So. You intend to hold the universe to ransom." Get used to this, Doctor. Just...get used to this.

The Master's putting an interesting spin on the "come to the Dark Side, we have cookies" speech right here:

He seems to be saying "come on, Doctor, let's play Overlords together! I'll be the evil overlord and you can be the good overlord!"

Actually, never mind, the Master wants to be the Good Overlord too...but why?

You know, it's really intriguing seeing how the Master plus Three's cabin fever is started to form a legit conflict in the latter's mind.

I mean, first we had his ambiguous semi-departure in Axos, now he seems to be honestly considering the Master's offer of half the universe.

Awww, come on, you had SUCH a perfect opportunity for an "all these corridors look the same" joke and you missed it!

Also, I love how the Master sounds so genuinely confused about WHY Three is adamantly turning down his offer.

Roger Delgado Appreciation Post: his eyes right now are just screaming "DOCTOR. SHUT. YOUR. FACE."

"Unhappiness and destruction?" Somehow I think destruction would come with something a bit more extreme than "unhappiness." Like "death."

"Not only does justice prevail on your planet sir, but also infinite compassion." Such a Three way of saying "you're cool, bro, I like you."

Wait so Three just set a giant weapon to self-destruct with a bunch of people still inside why would you do that.

"You'd better do something, Doctor. They're going to kill you!" Said...the Master, oddly enough.

COLONIST RESISTANCE ARMY! THEY LIVED!

"The Master! He's gone!" Well, he had the perfect cover of a bullet storm and a getaway car. What did you expect?

Well, the plot's wrapped up, the bad guys are taken care of, and you know what that means: time for the TARDIS to be conveniently found!

Meanwhile, back on Earth... "Doctor...come back at once." Or, That Awkward Moment When the Brig Summoned the TARDIS.

Awww, it really is like they never left.

Originally Posted April 7th, 2012

THE DAEMONS

Written by Robert Sloman and Barry Letts as "Guy Leopold"
Aired: May 22 – June 19, 1971

It Was a Dark and Stormy Night, because how else do you open a story called "The Daemons?"

JFC, guys, there's a difference between "dark and stormy" and "incoming hurricane."

And there goes our Poor Unfortunate Sap Who Dies Two Minutes Into The First Episode.

Huh, I'm not sure if this is supposed to be an archeological dig or a film set.

"But it really IS the dawning of the Age of Aquarius!" Also, hi Jo!

We're literally less than 3 minutes in and nearly every single character we've seen has been all "OMG MAGIC AND DOOM YOU GUYS AKASFHLDS."

In other news HOLY SHIT BESSIE IS ALIVE.

Or just remote-controlled by the Doctor to prove a point to Jo about magic. Okay, that works too.

A show about opening a burial chamber? So I guess it was a TV set AND an archeological dig.

Also, I think this is the first time in a while we've seen Three without a smoking jacket, or at least something velvet.

Never mind, there's the red jacket. Also, hi Yates!

And there's the BBC going meta again and talking about itself on one of its shows.

Cutting into the barrow "as if it were a giant pie."
#ASIFITWEREAGIANTPIE

Benton! We're still missing the Brig, but other than that the gang's all here!

Ah, Beltane. An event I hear about from a bunch of my friends up-state but I've never actually been to myself.

Hawthorne is going to be our token Local Prophet Who No One Listens To But Is Still Right in this story, isn't she?

Actually, I'm not sure why that's even a question. She is. She just is.

Okay, not a prophet but a white witch. This'll be interesting.

It seems that Three has either changed his mind about magic or sees science that needs to be done.

So after that cutaway to the local pub, I honestly have to wonder if we'll ever see any of those characters ever again.

Wait there was wind and the cop tried to stone the witch and then she embraced the wind and made it stop and he put the rock down and what.

Hey, hey guys, remember that time that the Master decided that putting on glasses would be a great disguise?
#seriouslywhatisonyourfacesir

Not sure why I'm so conscious of it this serial, but everyone's outfits and accessories look even more '70s than usual.

OH MY GOD NEVER MIND THE MASTER'S GLASSES *BRIG* WHAT ARE YOU WEARING.

Aww, poor Benton wants to go to the party but only the Brig gets to wear the fancy suit. Also, Sergeant is disappointed in sandwiches.

Hawthorne appears to be resistant to the Master's hypno-gaze. I'm liking this woman more and more with every scene.

Script for the Master's Fingers: "Snap! Hail Satan! Sic 'em, boy!"

I love how Benton starts off calling Yates "sir," but 10 seconds later they're chumming around about the football highlights. #UNITfamily

I think that's the first time I've heard Three accused of wearing a wig. (Seriously, where did that come from?)

They're doing the ceremony already? Huh, I thought this would be the climactic scene of the serial, not the first episode.

I'm trying really hard to not say that the Master's demon summoning looks more like a half-hearted LARP. Really. Hard.

Don'tcha hate it when you pull a boulder down in a cave and a huge snowstorm comes out? Me too.

Meanwhile back at UNIT HQ, we interrupt Happy Funtiems With Benton and Yates to bring you a special broadcast of Jo Grant Crying In A Cave.

I think this is the first time the Master's actually thanked someone for responding to "you will obey me." (Not in as many words, but still)

Yikes. So Three wasn't just slightly buried, but he appears to be *frozen solid.*

Aaaand then we cut to Benton, Yates, and Random Dude #3 all on the phone at once with jaunty elevator music in the background. ...Okay.

Ah yes, the traditional Doctor Gets Examined By Another Doctor Who Thinks He Surely Must Be Hearing Things When He Finds The Second Heart.

"Cheer up. While there's life, there's hope, right?" #eerilyprophetic-words

Also, "we've been cut off" has never been quite so literal. Someone just took what looked like a butcher knife to the telephone wire.

On a completely unrelated note, I REALLY love Jo's outfit in this serial. It almost makes her look like a blonde Sarah Jane.

Can I just take a moment to appreciate the fact that the helicopter says "G-UNIT" in big letters on the front.

"Come on, first thing's first."
"What? Like breakfast, you mean, sir?"
Benton. BENTON. I love you.

Oh wow. I would not be remotely surprised if the A-Team theme started playing over that shot of Benton and Yates getting out of the chopper.

And of course that U-Team video seems to have vanished from YouTube. Balls, I loved that mashup.

Usually when I watch McCoy-era Who, I feel like the '80s is radiating off the screen. Here, I can feel the '70s radiating off the screen.

Suddenly, Brig in bed. Oh my god why can't I stop laughing. "MY HELICOPTER?!?"

Cut from Brig in a bed to Benton saving a woman from a box. Because why not.

Also, I kind of love how Hawthorne has taken the most instant of instant shines to Benton.

Okay, does that design on the ground look like an archaic Trivial Pursuit board to anyone else?

Look dude, when you tell Benton to "move," he'll move, but not in the way you want him to. He will "move" his foot to your face.

Boy, that round orange filter over the camera lens sure does love chasing our heroes around the churchyard, doesn't it?

Also disintegrating people and setting things on fire and causing earthquakes and oh my god seriously what is happening. #hellbrokeloose

"...EUREKA!!!" On the plus side, hi Three, nice to see you awake again.

...That guy's van just exploded for no apparent reason. At least it had the courtesy to scare him away before going up in flames.

"Oh dear, you're a very heavy young man." Well, now Hawthorne has returned the favor and saved Benton.

Hannah J. Rothman

"Jo, did you fail Latin as well as science? Magister is the Latin word for Master!" Three sees through your cellophane-thin disguise, Master.

Brig's back! And it looks like the van blew for a reason. There seems to be a forcefield up that makes fire happen to whatever touches it.

Or it could be a heat barrier, that too.

"I see, Yates. So the Doctor was frozen stiff at the barrow and was then revived by a freak heat wave. Benton was beaten up by invisible forces and the local white witch claims she's seen the devil."
"Yes sir. I know it sounds a bit wild."
"It does indeed, Yates."

Okay. I love, LOVE how the Brig is completely stonefaced for all of that but then puts on his determinedface when he hears about the Master.

...Does that sign say "Nothing in my hand trinity?"

"If my theory is right, we're all in mortal danger."
"Everyone in the village?"
"Everyone in the whole world."
As per usual.

Damn gargoyles, always jumping into tunnels and ruining our exposition.

Unless I'm mistaken, Three just repelled a monster with a random incantation and a small garden trowel.

There's a "books! Greatest weapon in the world!" reference here somewhere.

So I'm not quite sure if Three just said that the "devil" was a creature from another world or that EVERYTHING with horns was an alien.

And we have our explanation. And it's more or less exactly what I expected it to be.

sigh Okay, I have to say I'm really not fond of plots with a "this species was crucial to the development of human civilization" twist.

Naturally Three's immediate reaction to the Brig's plan of "we will shoot at it" is "no, stop, stop saying words."

66

"I'm not going to sit here like a spare.........like a spare lemon..."
#likeasparelemon #thebrigisnowalemon

Suddenly ALL OF THE TECHNOBABBLE.

What was that smirk for Bentoooon, c'monnnnnn, tell ussssss...

whisper whisper whisper *scheme scheme scheme*

The Master seems to have reached full-on Bond-villain-with-a-god-complex mode here.

Also, I love how Bok is basically the Master's Pokémon.

Yates is straight-up PUNCHING THIS DUDE IN THE FACE REPEATEDLY and it is having absolutely no effect. Just...just wow.

Yates...that's a handgun. Somehow I don't think you can shoot down a helicopter with that.

Motorcycle Yates! Also, if the guy in the helicopter is trying to pull a kamikaze on Three and Jo, he's REALLY bad at aiming at the ground.

Suddenly A CHASE SCENE!

And there goes the chopper right into the heat barrier.

Motorcycle Three! Pertwee must've had fun making this serial.

I wonder if the UNIT tech guy with the glasses was any kind of precursor to Malcolm Taylor in Planet of the Dead.

Granted, they act nothing alike, but they look a bit similar and have similar UNIT positions.

WOW. I've seen Delgado!Master look concerned and angry before, but here he's in full-on HOLY SHIT WHAT HAVE I DONE mode.

Richard Franklin and the others must've had fun throwing themselves around the set like that.

I have a sneaking suspicion that Jo's about to sneak out of the window since she can't go down the stairs.
(Ack, no pun intended. But yes, it seems I was right.)

Also, I was going to mention this a while ago, but I love how the tavern's name is The Cloven Hoof.

"Reverse it."
"Reverse what?"
"Reverse the polarity!"

Okay...I'm sorry, but after all this build-up to the reveal of the Daemon himself, he looks like he's standing on giant chicken legs.

I am suddenly rather intrigued by the very visible vein on the side of Delgado's head.

Um, Master, with all due respect to your ego, who said anything about Earth or satanic powers being "rightfully yours?"

This scene is making me unimpressed with the Daemon itself, but VERY impressed with the fact that Delgado is BARELY BLINKING AT ALL.

Seriously, I've been watching his eyes and *they are barely moving.*

So Yates, you chose now to go and check up on Jo and not the last time the heatwave struck? Oh right, because the plot.

I'm surprised Benton's still calling him "sir" at this stage, considering they're out of uniform the situation doesn't call for formalities.

Then again, that's probably Tumblr imprinting a slightly different (and more casual) image of the UNIT Family in my brain.

Now we can add "motorcycle windshield" to the list of Things The Doctor Improvises As Science-Diagram-Explaining Surfaces.

"You know, Sergent, I sometimes wish I worked in a bank."

Ouch. Yates, I thought you liked Jo, stop calling her an idiot so much.

Huh. According to the InfoText, Pertwee had a stunt double. Considering how action-oriented he was, I'm a little surprised.

Come on, Benton, you've had a rough day. Sit down for a minute and let the nice witch make you some tea.

Suddenly...accordions? ...Sure, why not...?
The Maypole is the only thing that makes sense in this scene right now. I just...what...?

I can barely put this into words. There's cricketers(?) dancing with sticks that aren't bats and a man in half a chicken suit made of paper.

And they're all dancing.

MORRIS DANCERS. Suddenly everything makes sense.

And now Yates is dancing around the Maypole and Three's being held at gunpoint and stickpoint and I can't even this scene you guys.

Okay, maybe that wasn't Yates.

Tying Three up in the Maypole? OH how DASTARDLY.

That One Time Benton Was Attacked By A Morris Dancer And Was Saved By A Witch And Her Handbag.

That Other Time The Doctor Was Accused Of Being A Witch And Was Tied To A Maypole Presumably For The Sake Of Burning.

"You would dare to harm the great Wizard Qui Quae Quod?" #whyhappening

Thanks to the InfoText I know what that means, but still...

Some say "the secret to your power was inside you the whole time," but for Qui Quae Quod's "magic," it was made of pure Benton.

Also Bessie. (Guys. Guys why is everything in this scene wonderful.)

Just for good measure, That One Time Jo Grant Blew Her Cover To Save An Innocent Chicken.

Again, my apologies, but I really feel like Azal is the K-1 robot of the Pertwee era. It just...doesn't work.

When the only guy trying to yell the crowd into submission is wearing a paper-clippings suit, I don't think that's going to work.

On that note, pipe down, everyone, Three has a science lesson for you.

...and now I'm left to ponder the horrible implications of how exactly they got Jo into that dress.

Advantage of being a UNIT agent in plainclothes: enemies won't suspect that just tying your hands behind your back will get you to stay put.

I love how Bok doesn't even really need to *do* anything to keep people out of the cavern, he just needs to stand with his arms crossed.

(No seriously, he's just standing there like "bitch, *please.*")

And now newspaper-chicken-suit-man is no more.

Now one of the Master's Faceless Dudes In Cloaks seems to be waking up to the situation, which might be nicer if we knew who he was.

Somewheeeere uuunder the raaaaainbowwwww, the Briiiig wiiiiill riiiiiide...

So naturally JUST after they get the epic Daemon-breaking machine through the heat barrier, it explodes. Naturally.

Aww, poor Bok is reduced to stumbling around like a drunk and can't catch that damn kid on his lawn, I mean, the Doctor.

"...What in the blazes is that. Some kind of ornament?" Brig. Never stop saying things. Ever.

Speaking of which... "Jenkins! Chap with the wings, there, five rounds rapid."

Huh. According to the InfoText, that line was almost cut but was ultimate saved by Barry Letts. Thank you, sir!

So I was wondering earlier if Azal was played by Stephen Thorne, which apparently he is. Weird, usually I love his hamtastic characters.

Three has Jo back, so now I can only assume he's going to try and talk Azal out of destroying Earth. Or something. He sure is talking.

Meanwhile, UNIT is doing what UNIT does best: emptying its full payload into a creature that only takes damage from Science.

And naturally Yates' reaction is "well, this is doing jack shit. Go grab a bigger gun."

I kinda love how the Master seems *physically incapable* of comprehending the fact that a giant alien monster won't do what he tells it to.

"Who else is there strong enough to give these humans the leadership they need?!"

"I seem to remember somebody else speaking like that. What was the bounder's name...Hitler. Yes, that's right, Adolf Hitler. Or was it Genghis Khan?"

So Azal has decided to pass on his power to the Doctor and not the Master. Neither of them are particularly pleased with this conclusion.

Oh. And for a second I actually thought that bazooka worked.

Ah, never mind, Azal changed his mind after all. Only six minutes left...how exactly are they going to resolve this?

Umm...so Jo committing an act of self-sacrifice causes Azal to brain-melt in DOES NOT COMPUTE. Well. I can't say I was expecting that.

("Jon Pertwee took the model Bok home and kept it in his garden as a quirky alternative to a gnome.") #thebestpeople

HAH! Apparently the shot of the church blowing up was so real that the BBC got complaints for "demolishing" it.

And now Benton has the Master at gunpoint. This must be an incredibly satisfying moment for UNIT.

So of COURSE the second Benton looks away, the Master clocks him in the face. And Three's more concerned about people not shooting Bessie.

"You want him to get away??"
"Don't worry, Bessie'll bring him back."
#SCIENCE

Well, at least the Master has the decency to come quietly. Of course, I think Delgado!Master had the most decency out of any other Master.

("Christopher Barry asked the villagers to boo the Master as he goes but the children liked him so much that they wanted to cheer instead.")

All together now: awwwwwwww...

"Sergeant, we must do the fertility dance to celebrate!" ......I'll just leave this here.

"Fancy a dance, Brigadier?"
"That's kind of you, Captain Yates. Think I'd rather have a pint."

Awwww, happy musical dancing ending!

Originally Posted June 3rd, 2012

DAY OF THE DALEKS

Written by Louis Marks
Aired: January 1-22, 1972

So we open in a mansion and...what's the point of holding a guy at gunpoint if you're just going to teleport away after five seconds?

Ah, that's the point: freaking the living daylights out of your target.

Cut to the Brig on the phone with the Minister of Defense. It's always weird being reminded that the Brig *does* actually have superiors.

Aw, Jo's such a doll in that cowgirl outfit. (Seriously she looks like 12.)

"This won't do at all." YEAH, I HAD A FEELING THAT DUPLICATES OF YOU AND JO RANDOMLY APPEARING "WOULDN'T DO," AS YOU PUT IT. #what

And then the Brig walks through that same blank, yellow doorway...so is he from another timeline too?

So I wonder if the politics of this serial were legitimate Cold War worries or just the writers operating on UNIT Time. Or both.

PPPFFFFFFFFTT, the camera angles they picked for the would-be assassin's face are just what.

Hello, Aliens of the Week. You're the Ogrons, aren't you? If shrunken heads were normal-sized and had bodies, they'd probably look like you.

Found: Dead body (x1)

Meanwhile in space...

Yep, these are the Ogrons. They kinda remind me of pre-Sontarans. Except I much prefer the Sontaran speech patterns.

"It's our duty to protect you!" Which is why we're pointing at you with the gun that some random nutter threatened you with. Clearly.

Okay, so the guy wasn't dead, he was just "severely injured."

"You say this wasn't made on Earth. Do you mean it comes from another planet?" A+ deduction skills, Brigadier. You win a gold star.

Oh. Actually it seems that it was made on Earth from Earth materials BY someone from another planet. Well then.

Benton has a captive on a stretcher simply vanish right in front of him. And yet all his expression says is "well...that happened...?"

"RE-PORT." Oh hi, Dalek!

"Jo? How would you like to spend the night in a haunted house?"
"O___O"

Three sitting down in a mansion with wine and fancy cheese. All he's missing is a pipe, a fireplace, and a pair of slippers.

Also his dialogue in this scene might as well be "BOY I SURE DO LOVE WINE. HEY JO DID I MENTION THIS IS GOOD WINE. BECAUSE IT IS GOOD WINE."

Is there a word for food-related cockblocking? Because that's what just happened between Benton and Yates. Poor Benton, he just wants foods.

You know, this whole bit with the Benton/Yates/food/wine has nothing to do with the plot, but I'm glad it's here. Adds a sweet familial touch.

I kinda love how Three is the more certain of the existence of ghosts but much calmer, while Jo is the opposite.

Um, Jo, I'm really not sure how you're asleep right now. That position looks kinda uncomfortable.

Poor Nameless UNIT Chaps, zapped by a ray gun that...sounds suspiciously like a Dalek gun...

WOAH. HOLD UP. IS THAT THE BRIG WITH HIS JACKET UNBUTTONED. IT IS, OH MY GOD.

Okay stop stop stop stop. You can't just throw WWIII at us with just one previous mention of it and no build-up. You're doing it wrong.

Looks like Three's got that little box up and working again. It sounds like a growling dog.

Hah, forget cheese, you know what else goes great with wine? Ass-kicking. #timefu

Well. I guess this is what everyone meant about the Dalek voices in this story. Gah.

(And before anyone asks, Netflix only sent me Disk 1 which doesn't have any of the special feature options for watching with the updates.)

The way these guys keep talking about the "twentieth century time zone" makes it feel like I'm watching The War Games in color.

Wow. They didn't even bother taking out the ending sting and start of the credits music from the last episode. Really?

For the briefest of seconds, I thought that dude in the black suit was Ainley!Master. No idea why, this guy's clean-shaven.

I was going to mention this last time and forgot: it's great to see a woman in charge of a field operation instead of sitting at a computer.

Said the woman sitting at a computer.

Apparently her name is Anat. She's pointing a gun at Three, but I already like her.

"It's none too warm a day, is it, sir?" Oh Benton, you wouldn't be saying that if you were where I am now. #epicamericaheatwave

Also, I would've thought you and Yates would be smart enough to check out that mysteriously slightly-open door just down the hall.

Yates, with due respect, I don't think the Brig would have a change of priority if Three and Jo went missing during an international crisis. Pertwee must've had fun trying to get that gag out of his mouth.

I know she was just trying to reach the ropes, but Jo rubbing her head against Three's back like that was just awwwww...

You know, I'm a bit surprised the Doctor doesn't meet people with amateur time machines trying to change the past more often.

"AC-TI-VATE. THE. MAG-NA-TRON." Oh, you mean that pair of big metal balls? Okay.

Maybe my understanding of military works is completely wrong, but...

...I find it odd that Benton and Yates, as commanding officers, do so much hands-on work themselves instead of sending scouts or something.

On the plus-side, it means more Favorite UNIT Chaps action for us at home.

Is that...*gasp* a BOMB in...*gasp* PLASTIC WRAP? #gasp

I wonder if the music reverb from the Ogron's hand-chop was meant to represent the ringing in that guy's ears after the impact. #idk

no seriously guys HOW DO YOU KEEP MISSING THAT DOOR

Can we all just give a round of applause for Nick Courtney's acting in this scene? Because seriously, this man is amazing.

The second Jo said "go back to September" my mind immediately jumped to 9/11. Then I remembered that hadn't happened yet.

So of COURSE Three gets cut off right before he gets to explain the Blinovitch Limitation Effect.

Brig's on his way and he knows something's up. I wonder if this will ultimately be a hindrance or a help to the situation.

Ouch. Jo finally gets her knots undone and it seems to be a rather inopportune moment for doing so.

Woah wait, so that...wait...that happened. Okay, Jo's on the enemy ship now. But she wasn't even pressing any buttons. How do.

Well at least the boss has the courtesy to offer her his chair. And I just remembered that this is only Jo's second trip through time. wait why does he suddenly remind me of @stephenfry in that Australian Soap sketch

Ahhhh I see what you did there. You asked Jo for the "exact date" but she still didn't give you the year. #UNITdatingatitsfinest

(and by finest I mean worst because you can't have an "exact date" without a year)

NO SERIOUSLY WHY DOES THIS GUY'S FACE REMIND ME OF STEPHEN FRY. He doesn't even have a crocked nose.

Also, I think it's time I mentioned: yes, the Dalek voices in this story ARE pretty bad. They all just sound remarkably uninterested.

Rather bold of Three to start cutting at his ropes while his captors were still leaving the room.

And I love how he prioritizes retrieving his cape over getting out before the aliens come in through the window.

Here we go: more material for the "but the Doctor would never use a gun!" crowd. Also, hi Brig! Good timing.

I love how the Brig doesn't even really make an effort to stop Three from taking his Jeep. Just a yell, a headshake, and that's it.

A wild DALEK appeared! What will DOCTOR 3 do?

Again, they didn't even bother taking the ending musical sting out. Huh.

DOCTOR 3 used RUN! It's not very effective...

"This may come as a shock to you, but you've just traveled two hundred years through time." Actually it won't. Because Doctor.

So I didn't realize this until after I'd finished the last episode, but isn't this the Daleks' first appearance in the show since Evil?

Considering that, I'm surprised they didn't give them a grander re-entrance.

A bit amused at how Jon Pertwee's hair kinda makes him look like a dirty blond in this light.

Either the Ogron's battle armor is REALLY loud, or that field of weeds is paved with broken glass. ALL of the broken glass.

The phrase "human guerrillas" just came up. It looks fine in writing, but try saying it out loud and see if it doesn't sound a bit odd.

In the meantime, hello Periscope With Mysterious Flashing Red Circles!

Now I'm honestly starting to wonder whether or not the women at the computers are supposed to be androids. They just...don't act human.

The fact that they all have shiny makeup doesn't hurt the android argument either.

How To Argue In The Future: sit down with your cohorts and bitch about the mission's failures while angrily smoking cigars.

Oh wow. When that third guy tried to shut them up with "both of you," it sounded distinctly like "no, fuck you" the first time. #iamtired

Slavery of the Future: people in potato sacks carrying small amounts of gravel in very shiny oversized trash cans. Well okay then.

So now I have to wonder if this guy is treating Jo so well in the interest of actually being nice or just as a cover-up.

It's probably the latter, but somehow I feel that this guy is actually trying to be a gentleman to her.

I don't know why I doubted myself: this guy is totally pulling a face and I don't know why I would think otherwise.

Especially since OH DEAR GOD THAT IS ONE OF THE CREEPIEST SMILES I'VE EVER SEEN.

Three is tied up and there's jacketless-ness, a whip, and an unbuttoned shirt involved. A bit kinky, methinks. :/

Ah. Forget what I said last episode about the women wearing shiny makeup. EVERYBODY in this time looks like that, apparently.

This is almost turning into Caves of Androzani. It seems like there's so many different sides that I don't who's working towards what anymore.

Also, we've only got about 30 minutes left in a Dalek story in which the Daleks have only had about 5 minutes of screentime. #huh

Well, at least Three and Jo have been reunited.

The controller seems to be going into retroactive pay-no-attention-to-the-man-behind-the-curtain mode now.

Also he really has Jo under his thumb, doesn't he? (And I just happened to pause on a nice "bitch *please*" reaction face from Three.)

Ah, finally we get a decent-sounded Dalek. And yes, it would appear that this is their first time seeing Three.

"WE WILL USE. THE MIND. A-NA-LY-SIS. MA-CHINE." #nonotthemindprobe

It's good to know that companion screams can still be put to practical use every once in a while. Also vases of wine.

Now THAT is the beefiest tricycle I've ever seen.

Even better: the InfoText identifies it as an "all-terrain motor tricycle." Does this count as Enhanced Childhood?

And of COURSE putting it in the show was Pertwee's idea. Of COURSE it was.

("Pertwee fell in love with the vehicle and had to be dragged away to continue filming.") Oh WOW. Actual Action Rider Jon Pertwee.

Apparently the Daleks didn't want to be bothered to make their own Doctor Who fanvid, so they just torrented one from ThreeTube.

I'd be lying if I said this image of Three lying *completely* motionless on the table wasn't more than a little unsettling.

I almost love how the Daleks' monotone makes their declaration of having taken over Earth and warped history seem rather casual.

And of course now Three is COMPLETELY recovered and shows absolutely no signs of having been half-dead just a couple scenes ago. Well.

So yeah, Two, what was that you were saying a while back about the late 20th century having "very few wars?"
(I could be remembering that completely wrong, though, so forgive me if I messed that up.)

So 'course I'm only JUST realizing that these guys are living in the post-apocalyptic world caused by WWIII from the first couple episodes.

You know, somehow I think those laser guns might be more effective if they actually, you know, shot lasers.

Oh right, I forgot, these guns don't really shoot, they dissolve.

I REALLY don't think the guerrillas have really stopped to think through the consequences of changing such a crucial point in history.

But never mind the impending war and horrible distortion of history, look at the funny running man with the wounded arm, kids!

Is this an impending Stable Time Loop I see coming up?

Aaaaaand NOW it finally dawns on everyone.

So it turns out Three sparing the controller's life paid off after all and now he's returned the favor. Awww.

And he even went back and lied to the Daleks faces and died anyway. Wow, I guess he was made of tougher stuff than I thought. Good show sir.

Hello, Actual BBC Presenter!

So here come our Token Representatives From Around The World and we only have 5 minutes to find and defuse a very literal war-starting bomb.

guys why are you having a Dalek invasion now I just said there's only five minutes left what are you doing

Three minutes left oh my god seriously how are they going to fix this.

For a supposed evacuation, everyone's moving rather slowly, aren't they?

Ah, so THAT'S how they're going to resolve everything. Also, I think that's the first time I've ever seen a Dalek nudge open a patio door.

Well. Rather abrupt ending, but there you go, I suppose.

Originally Posted July 9th, 2012

THE CURSE OF PELADON

Written by Brian Hayles
Aired: January 29 – February 19, 1972

So we open on...a Transylvanian castle on a mountainside with Roman guards. Interesting choice.

Our two black-and-purple-robed fellows look like they could be twins...except one's about a full foot taller than the other.

Ah, so they *are* brothers! And their leader (their king?) bears a striking resemblance to Hugh Laurie's vengeful German from Blackadder II.

Okay, let's see if I can keep this straight: Torbis is the shorter one and Hepesh is the taller one. AND THE KING IS DAVID TROUGHTON.

...oh. Maybe I don't need to keep track of who's who because I think Torbis just got axed by our Fursuit Monster of the Week.

TARDIS! And the landing sound keeps looping...

"This is the TARDIS' first test flight since I got it working again." ...I don't remember anything about that from last time...

"You said we'd only be a few minutes, right?" Oh. Oh Jo Grant you precious innocent fluffy bunny. No. No, this is going to take 4 episodes.

Jo does look adorable in this episode, though. Although it looks like she really overdid the eyeshadow.

"Perfect landing." If "perfect landing" means "teetering precariously on the edge of a cliff," yes, that is a perfect landing.

Well, now we know how the TARDIS is made inaccessible for the rest of the story. Poor girl, though. That model took quite a tumble.

hoLY CHRISTMONKEYS ALPHA CENTAURI

I mean it was already great that he's a giant green penis in a cape but then he stARTED TALKING AND

SERIOUSLY I HOPE THAT SQUEAK I JUST MADE DIDN'T WAKE UP MY PARENTS

It is going to be physically impossible for me to take any scenes with this character seriously. And I'm okay with that.

"This is not a matter to trouble the delegates!" Sure our chancellor was just slain by a mythical monster but DON'T WORRY WE GOT THIS.

Can we please take a moment to give Jo Grant All of the Awards for mountain climbing in heels and a dress with no safety harness.

Although I would give the production team Fewer Awards for not dubbing her lines in very well in this scene.

I should probably mention here that this is my first time watching a Pertwee story after listening to Lis Sladen's autobiography.

She included an anecdote from the first time she met Pertwee after being cast as Sarah Jane, and it was rather heart-stabby.

Lis had been warned beforehand that Jon was still sad about Katy leaving, but Lis was naturally determined to make her own impression.

So he calls her over at a cast-and-crew pub meet, they get properly introduced...and he says "What would you like to drink, Katy?"

And then he stopped and realized what he'd said and just burst into tears. So seeing him and Jo together might make me sad now.

Anyway, sorry for the detour. Back to Peladon...

Jo Grant found Tunnel (x1)!

That's...an interesting design for the delegate from Arcturus. He has a dome over his head like one of those fountain-drink-mixers.

You know, the ones where it's in a plastic box and there's a jet of drink spraying onto the ceiling and down the sides? Yeah, like that.

Except instead of lemonade, it's green slime. Sooooo...

ALSO BASED ON THEIR SHAPE AND FIREPOWER THEY MAY VERY WELL BE RELATED TO DALEKS. SO THERE'S THAT.

Jade statue of a man-pig? Jade statue of a man-pig.

It might help if every scene with King Peladon didn't make me go "OH NO HE'S HOT" every few seconds. It's a tad frustrating.

Interesting. Apparently Peladon's father was a pure-blooded king, but his mother was from Earth. I wonder how far in the future this is?

I think it was Nash's video about The Happiness Patrol that talked about this story being an allegory for the UK joining the EU...

...and yeah, it's...it's really showing now.

Hmm. I wonder if this cave set was reused from The Silurians. It looks really familiar.

Also, I'll bet that Three and Jo are going to show up at the palace and get blamed for Torbis' death. Because that usually happens.

"Eeny meeny miney mo..."
RAAAWWWRR
"...Miney?"
nod

"Oh no, it's blocked up." Rather casual reaction when you can still hear that monster roaring, Jo.

ICE WARRIOR! I forgot they were in this story!

I kinda want to give Alpha Centauri a pat on the head and a biscuit. Seriously, he has the cutest, most delightfully out-of-place voice.

"For that day, a stranger will appear in the land, bringing peril to Peladon and great tribulation to its king."
Three and Jo enter

GEE WHO COULD'VE POSSIBLY SEEN THIS COMING

Oh wait, never mind. The Ice Warriors think they're the delegates from Earth.

So to make things weirder, I just realized that Alpha Centauri's cape kinda looks like a broken condom. #costumingjustcantwin

So apparently only "men of rank" and "females of royal blood" are allowed in the throne room. Pretty Princess Jo!

Woah. Never mind. QUEEN Jo. She just seized the moment by the balls.

"May I present Her Royal Highness, Princess Josephine." No…Three, we just established, Jo is QUEEN. #allhailqueenjo

Queen Jo OF TARDIS.

"The whole affair was most deplorable. The pilot was exceedingly inefficient." And there goes Three with his gurl-what-you-say face.

Poor King Peladon, he just wants people to stop reminding him that his friend just got murdered.

They keep calling Three "Chairman Delegate" but it always sounds like "German Delegate."

Jo, are you having an oh-no-he's-hot moment too? Because King Peladon says he wants to speak to you again "less formally."

Uh oh, down comes a sabotaged statue! Rather silently, too. I'm pretty sure stone creaks and cracks when it falls over.

We now return to I Still Can't Get Over Alpha Centauri's Voice Oh My God

"We come to help your people! To raise them from barbarism!"

...Wait, so is this less about the EU and more about White Savior Complex?

"Maybe they don't want to be raised!" Maybe I was right. Well then.

You can tell it's the 70s because even alien kings are wearing mini-skirts. #kingpeladon #wecanseeyourthighs

Aaaaand no one saw Queen Jo sneaking off? No one? ...Okay.

Also, is it just me, or did they later recycle Hepesh's robes into Romana's dress from Androids of Tara?

3...2...1...CUE FLIRTING!

"I was brought up by wise old men. I hardly ever see anyone young... and...beautiful..." #nowkiss

Um...okay that just got Oedipal really fast. Peladon says he and Jo "share a bond" because...his mother was an Earth woman. Ummmm.

Speaking of which, why does that one guard kinda look like Benton as a half-naked Centurion?

"Well YOU managed to slip away without anybody noticing, remember?" Huh. I wasn't expecting them to actually bring that up.

Wow. I think this is the first time they've addressed the issue of aliens outside the gender binary on this show.

Jo Grant is such a cutie-patootie I can't...

seriously I can feel the adorable radiating off the screen

Can we talk about the lighting in this scene with Three confronting the Ice Warriors? Because his face is mostly in shadow and it's spooky.

Also, that was the first time I was ever able to catch a glimpse of the actor's eyes through the red lenses. Pretty tough, though.

I can tell these are friendlier Ice Warriors because they haven't shot anyone yet, even when they find Jo rummaging through their stuff.

So Earth is being treated as an unwanted meddling agent. Which makes me wonder if it's the America analog of this piece.

For anyone doubting that Jo Grant is a badass, I humbly direct you to this scene. #escapingthroughawindow #inheelsandadress

The InfoText talks about the folks in Children's Programming at the BBC finding this serial "a little horrific, with a nightmarish quality."

And this happens RIGHT when we get easily the scariest image in the story so far. So...a "little" horrific feels a bit of an understatement.

It also talks about how this story had some of the highest viewing numbers since Galaxy 4, which makes me wonder...Galaxy 4? Really?

"But the Doctor did say you're a race of warriors!"
"We were, once. But now we reject violence!"

I have to admit, the idea of Ice Warriors "rejecting violence" feels like a pretty strong contradiction in terms.

Yikes. I don't remember the last time I saw someone flip out this hard over someone touching their statue.

And of COURSE the next scene is basically "you touched the thing. THE ONLY PUNISHMENT IS DEATH."

Sounds like Hepesh is barely beating around the bush anymore. He just wants Three dead by this point.

And now it's time for Convenient Loopholes! Good thing Trial By Combat sounds right up Three's alley.

So he'll have to fight Half-Naked Roman Benton (turns out his name is Grun) which is a tad problematic considering he's...well...a good guy.

King Peladon finally asked Jo outright to marry him. Well that only took forever.

It's also worth mentioning that she doesn't seem to be taking this very well.

Cut to Three lying sprawled out on a bed with his velvet jacket lying open. #ohnoheshot

"I don't want your death! Trust me!"
dramatic music cue

suspicious look
Hepesh, are you even trying?

Oh. Hepesh just outlined a map of the secret tunnels for Three and basically said "here's your way out, bro." Okay then.

Pretty sure that's the first time I've ever seen a companion shove two Ice Warriors aside, out of frustration, just to get past them.

Next on the Doctor's tinkering list: an oversized dental mirror. That causes dizziness, apparently.

Still trying to figure out if I find benevolent Ice Warriors to be weird or a pleasant change.

"Do you remember when that statue fell? The Doctor saved my life. Now I intend to save his." Made up my mind: pleasant change.

Now I get to wonder if Arcturus is a villain or just a douchebag.

cue Secret Tunnel song from Avatar

Awwww, lookit the big fuzzy pig monster!

Aggedor, I presume? *scratches behind the ears*

Aww, this must be Three's Venusian Lullaby! Naptime for Aggedor. :3

And the InfoText confirms my suspicion that Pertwee was singing it roughly to the tune of God Rest Ye Merry Gentleman.

Fun fact: that's easily one of my favorite Christmas carols.

Okay, maybe not naptime just yet. Hey Jo, think you can lend a hand?

Umm, well chasing a monster off with fire wasn't quite what Three had in mind, but okay.

Bits of heart melting onto the floor because Three and Jo's adorableness is just too much.

"No one sees Aggedor and lives!"
"Well we just did! And I must say he's quite pleasant company, for an animal. He didn't even seem to mind when I scratched him behind the ears."

That rare moment when my Aww towards a monster becomes canonical.

So apparently being "lowered into the pit" on Peladon literally means "climb down this rope into the pit."

Time for spear-fighting! Also, there's a noticeable difference between the filmed fight sequence and the videotaped viewing sequence.

What's happening to Three's spear right now feels a lot like the stick fight in Men in Tights where the sticks keep breaking and shrinking.

Welp. I guess Arcturus was just being a substitute Dalek after all. I wonder if he and Hepesh were in cahoots this whole time.

I was right! Although I wasn't expecting Arcturus to get blown up less than a minute into the last episode. That...eww.

Usually we reach this degree of plot resolution with ten minutes left to go...so are they only Hepesh-hunting for the whole last episode?

Nope, first we must have POLITICS!

Not sure what Grun's up to. Is he trying to release Aggedor? What was he signalling to Three earlier? Who knows? Who knows. #imalmostsorry

I ADORE how Three tells Jo to take an active political role on her own and she doubts nothing. Say what you want, but girl's got brains.

Also, Grun doesn't even have dialogue and he still manages to be one of the most awesome characters in this serial.

...I said literally seconds before Hepesh took him down with no effort.

No really can we talk about Jo Grant and how she got the Federation council to come to a unanimous decision because

Sooo...either the Ice Warriors have their info wrong or King Peladon ignored Jo's proposal rejection and went "no, I want one anyway."

I know it was just the Warriors' hissing, but that sound on the discovery of the broken communicator should've been followed by "well shit."

There's a friendzone joke in here somewhere, but I do honestly think Peladon's trying to be a nice guy and not a Nice Guy.

Yes, we get it: Hepesh did the thing.

Also, now I understand why Alpha Centauri is always called a NERVOUS penis in a cape. Gurl/boi, calm yo tits.

Meanwhile, fighting ensues between two factions of half-naked men in purple mini-skirts! #ihavenothingtocomplainabouthere

Grun is great. Aggedor is great. SO MUCH OF THIS SERIAL'S CAST IS GREAT.

Now that we finally see Aggedor in a room full of people, I finally notice how...short...he is...?

Hepesh is going to die in Peladon's arms, isn't he?

Yup. And his dying words to his king were basically "welp, I done goofed. Peace out."

I was going to mention this earlier, but Peladon seems to keep the exact same expression for the entire story...

...and he only seems to be changing it just now, after the death of the man who nearly killed him. Dude.

Off-handed mention that the Time Lords were just fucking around with Three again, and then hello Aggedor!

guys he's rubbing up against three like a giant dog and he's growling affectionately and everything oh my god

One last hurrah before the crew departs, Peladon? Nice giant jewel-encrusted ruff, by the way.

"I need you."
"But you don't understand! I'm not even a real princess!"
"That doesn't matter."
#NOW #KISS

"I'll talk to you again after the coronation." and there goes my heart

AND THEY FINALLY FUCKING KISSED

I seriously don't remember the last time I shipped a companion and a one-off character this hard. This tops Leela and Andred by miles.

Ah, I was wondering when the real Earth delegate would arrive. "Doctor? What doctor? Doctor who?" #yousaidthething

And they need to bid a hasty retreat and miss the coronation after all. *casually throws self off a cliff*

Although the Earth delegate's reaction to the TARDIS vanishing at the very end was pretty excellent.

BUT WAIT I GOT THROUGH THAT ENTIRE LAST EPISODE AND ONLY JUST FIGURED OUT: "AGGEDORABLE"

Originally Posted July 2nd, 2013

THE SEA DEVILS

Written by Malcolm Hulke
Aired: February 26 – April 1, 1972

Wow. No delay in getting to the action. LITERALLY the first thing we see is a sailor calling Mayday and people screaming in the background.

Hello again, Jo! Nice to see you again!

"There you are, Jo! That's the Master's permanent residence from now on!" ...Wait, WHEN did he get locked up in a seaside castle?

obligatory checking of Wikipedia Ah yes, there were only a couple serials between this and The Daemons.

DELGADO!MASTER! I think I've waited too long for this.

Although that Extreme Close-up could've waited a while longer...

Swords. I see them. On the wall. I know where this thread is going. ...seriously, what prison keeps SWORDS on its walls?

Ah, so there were days when the Doctor and the Master (and Jo, apparently) could engage in legitimately casual chit-chat.

"Changed men" don't have evil laughs. But then again, we all knew that. And we all know that Three knows that.

"Well, he used to be a friend of mine once. A very good friend. In fact, you might almost say we were at school together." D'awwww...

And why did those lines feel strangely evocative of Obi-Wan talking about Anakin in the original Star Wars? It hadn't even been made yet.

So the Master wants a color...sorry...colour TV for his room? I wonder where this is going...

Hey, look at Three! He's *insert obligatory stupid "I'm on a Boat" reference here*

Guys, I really don't understand what the Master's strange obsession with children's television is. First Teletubbies, now these aardvarks.

So apparently Jo Grant + motorcycle = access to anywhere.

And then they heard a s'plosion!

I knew the Sea Devil's costumes were...not what the crew had planned, but...bright blue mesh bathrobes? Really?

Seaman!Master! ...I mean, Navy!Master! *facepalm*

Huh. He seems to be having a bad hypnotism day. Solution? Karate-chop to the back of the neck.

So the plot thread with the Master and the plot thread with the Sea Devils feel almost completely separate. Really, guys?

Oh wait, they did say that this was how Malcolm Hulke wrote stories...

CRAP. Just missed my 2,000th Tweet. This is my 2,002nd.

How do you pass the time while waiting for guards to check on your imprisoned nemesis? Play blindfolded golf indoors, of course!

SWORD FIGHT. SWORD FIIIIIIIGHT. Also, I coulda sworn Three just yelled something in Japanese.

Im in ur prison sell, noming ur sammich.

Im in mah prison sell, stabbin ur bax.

YES THE BEGINNING OF THE NEXT EPISODE IS RECAP-PING THE WHOLE FIGHT SCENE.

Wow. Jo made surprisingly good work of, what appear to be, full-trained prison personnel.

Seriously, what is it with trained armed guards and their regular failure to hold their own against the Doctor's companions?

Don't bother the Master now. He's making a SCIENCE.

uncuffs Three's left hand
"How very kind of you."
cuffs Three's right hand to the chair
"How very UNkind of you."

NOW the two plot threads come together.

Hey...um...any chance you could translate what Jo just mimed to us through the window?

Impressively sneaky Jo is impressively sneaky.

And sinking submarine is sinking.

KNOCK *KNOCK* *KNOCK*
"There's something out there, sir..."

Guns all around, minefield below, Sea Devils on the tide...Three and Jo are literally surrounded from EVERY side except up.

Wait, WHY did Three fall over, what appeared to be, the same fence twice?

Also, the music in this serial is so electronic that I can barely tell the soundtrack from the sound effects.

The men in the submarine are...cooperating cordially with the Sea Devil? I wonder how they're going to explain this...

Okay, Three, I can understand stealing the Master's delicious sammich, but...stealing your companion's delicious sammich? Really?

So what's the betting they're going to open that diving tank and find Three not-being-in-it?

Called it.

So we finally get to hear the Sea Devils speak. And talks between them and Three seem to be more tense and hostile than last time.

Why do I have a feeling that EVERY Silurian-related plot is going to be the same "why can't you share Earth with humans" deal?

The original The Silurians was like this, The Hungry Earth/Cold Blood was like this, this is like this...

Then again, this and The Silurians were written by the same guy. Warriors of the Deep wasn't, but it had Silurians AND Sea Devils.

AND TURLOUGH. MORE INCENTIVE FOR ME TO WATCH IT.

"NO! The Doctor is your deadly enemy! He must be DE-STROYED!" Oh yes, The Silurians also didn't have the Master pulling the strings.

So I can't help but wonder whether or not that's stock footage of the Naval fleet swarming in.

I think it's been made quite clear now that ALL hibernation units are faulty.

The Slow-Motion Diplomatic High-Five of Hey-Why-Don't-We-Try-Peace!

AQUA-SPLOSIONS.

And Three escapes! Only for his ex-captors to be rock-crushed. So he goes back to...get their gun?

RETURN OF WINDOW-PERTWEE.

What do you do when you're being held captive in your own submarine by sea monsters? Play a happy game of cards, of course!

"They're holding us back with some kind of forcefield!" Okay, so how did it move again RIGHT after you said that?

Back to the surface! This calls for the ORANGE MUG OF VIC-TORY!

"Our duty is to destroy the Queen's enemies. Don't you know your national anthem?" Makes me wonder, DOES Gallifrey have a national anthem?

"But the point, Mr. Parliamentary Private Secretary, is that you have

NOT destroyed. You have just made them ANGRY. VERY. VERY. ANGRY."

Holy balls, guys, intense Pertwee is INTENSE.

YES. IS CAN BE TIME-FU TIEMS NAO.

And...that was fast. For a second I thought Three's face was melting/deflating/something.

So I wonder if Three's actually trying to sabotage the Master's device instead of fixing it. If he is, why hasn't the Master caught it yet?

Unless this is establishing that the Doctor IS, in fact, the superior technomancer.

I KNEW IT. JO IS WEARING HEELS. Shorter heels that other companion's I've seen but STILL SHE'S WEARING HEELS.

Awww, Doctor and Master, makin' a science together...

Okay, Three, I saw how you gripped the Master's lower abs just now. And you need a "polarizing condenser"? Planning on reversing something?

"Don't worry about the guards, you leave them to me." Please tell me this implies more impending Time-Fu.

Okay, I guess it didn't. High-frequency pulsation noise is what we get instead.

ALSO JO PILOTING SOME SORT OF LAND-AND-SEA CRAFT.

It's time for another round of Gunning Down Slimy Things!

Three, I know you're in a rush here but...leaving a soldier alone with the Master WITHOUT warning him about the hypnotism? Really?

SEE? SEE? Also, WHY DO THINGS APPEAR TO BE ON FIRE?

PLEASE TELL ME THERE'S GOING TO BE A DOCTOR VS. MASTER BOAT CHASE SCENE HERE.

THERE IS. Oh man, Jon Pertwee must've had fun filming this...

Wait, the Sea Devils only brought one transport pod, but both Three AND the Master are down in the base now. Must've been a tight fit...

"Before you activated it, I reversed the polarity of the neutron flow." And if I remember right, this is the only time he ACTUALLY says it.

I'm sorry, it needs to be said again: "Before you activated it, I reversed the polarity of the neutron flow."

So the Doctor and the Master are locked in a cell together and there's about to be an epic s'plosion. Anything could happen now...

Wait wait wait WHAT? Did I miss something MAJOR? The cell door's magically open now and...WHAT? This has to be a mistake in the video.

tries to check Crap, screwed that up. Gimme a few more minutes...

So the video somehow skipped Three sonicing them out. Found it on another vid. Come on guys, that was important!

Guys, the Master in a bright orange inflatable wetsuit waving to a hovercraft has to be seen to be believed.

And then he suddenly collapses? Wonder if he's got the bends or something...

...actually it's probably just a ruse to escape once they get to shore. Then again, he's at a naval base. How's he going to escape?

Unless he hijacks the ambulance or something...

WAIT. A. FUCKING. SECOND. SINCE WHEN DOES THE MASTER CARRY RUBBER MASKS OF HIMSELF TO DISGUISE OTHER PEOPLE AS HIM. THAT...I DON'T EVEN...

Though for all intents and purposes, giving someone a you-mask and riding off in a hovercraft is a pretty damn awesome mode of escape.

And I was right earlier, that WAS stock footage of the Navy ships.

Originally Posted June 2nd, 2010

THE MUTANTS

Written by Bob Baker and Dave Martin
Aired: April 8 – May 13, 1972

First guy we see appears to have escaped from a medieval dungeon and is...growing stegosaurus spines out of his back.

Going out on a limb here, but I'm juuuuust going to assume that maybe perhaps he's one of the titular Mutants. Probably. #ofcourseheis

Old Guy now being chased by Screaming Pudgy Guy.

Sorry Jo, looks like lunch'll have to wait, if that rocky egg thing that just randomly materialized on Three's workbench is any indication.

Also, I would recommend not suggesting that you eat it.

I ADORE how Jo's reaction to Three telling her to stay put is to tighten her jacket, yell "oh no you don't!" and rush into the TARDIS.

Speaking of Jo's jacket, I'm already digging her outfit in this story. Even the heeled boots look pretty boss.

Considering her "there's only one little planet I want to see" speech later, I'm a bit surprised at Jo's enthusiasm for being in space here.

Okay, so now I have to wonder if that K-9 font was the only font allowed in old TV sci-fi. Because it shows up here a LOT.

Unless these are two different races, I'm not sure why half these people look like Roman centurions and the other half are Made of Space.

Also, this is the second time in a row that I've used the centurion comparison, but I think it applies much better here than in Peladon.

Well, they keep talking about "my people," so I guess we are dealing with multiple races here.

And I'm glad to say that also means we have the pleasure of a not-completely-white cast for once!

I begin to sense that this story is going to have anti-colonialism overtones. And the Made of Space people are called the Overlords.

Aw, Three's trying to make a profound point about the nature of civilization but he's like "Jo stop laughing let me explain to you a thing."

So...I was about to say the alarm system sounded almost musical...but then I realized that was the actual soundtrack.

Welp, our heroes have been caught by the Overlords and Three has his best "well, shit" face on.

"Doctor, you can see the planet in daylight now."
"So you can."
...Actually, that looks like exactly the same footage clip you used earlier.

Wait a sec...that's supposed to be Earth? Also JO YOUR SUN-GLASSES.

Or maybe the planet below is Solos. I'm...really not sure.

And after a good long history lesson from the InfoText, it seems I was right about the colonialism allegory in this story...

...since Apartheid was still a major issue when this story came out. #themoreyouknow

So it would appear that the big guy with the 58 on his chest is our Douchebag de Jour.

Shooting the egg doesn't open it, but it does make it glow pretty colors. Also, I think it's the one providing the soundtrack.

Anyone else find it odd that there's a perfectly sized platform just standing there for the Marshal to mount and shoot the egg, though?

Oh lord, I REALLY hope the whole rest of this story isn't a prolonged game of Hot Potato with that egg until it opens.

In The Future, we won't be watching TV on Super Ultra 3D HD screens, but through large fairground crystal balls.

Aw, Three, did you really have to sleeper-hold that guy? He seemed nice. Oh well, an escape opportunity is an escape opportunity.

Sounds like they've moved on to the BY THE WAY DID WE MENTION THIS STORY HAS A MESSAGE ABOUT A TOPICAL ISSUE part of the serial.

Now I'm confused. Why are the Solonians chanting "FREEDOM" angrily when the Overlords have just said they're giving them their independence?

Oh good, the Hot Potato game seems to be ending here, now that Ky's touch has made it open.

The Administrator is played by Geoffrey Palmer! I KNEW that face looked absurdly familiar!

Oh wow, you weren't kidding about the Rick James thing. Although that wasn't THE Rick James.

Jo, didn't he JUST say that the atmosphere outside was toxic and that you wouldn't last outside without a mask?

Guards' abilities to fire from the ground after being strangled never fails to baffle me ever so slightly.

Good ol' Three. He's not even threatening out loud to punch the Marshall in the face but his face and tone suggest that he'd really like to.

Time for Carrying Jo Grant Through a Toxic Bog.

"I was rather hoping for a particle reversal set-up..." ...you know what, I don't even need to say it.

The Overlords have a weather control station? I have two theories, and one involves them being douchebags on an even more epic scale.

Hello, Random German! And his name is Jaeger. Funny this should come up the day after I almost saw Pacific Rim.

Again, not sure if I'm hearing the sound effects or the soundtrack.

The leader's son is in league with the Marshal to assassinate the Administrator... Welp, this is what I get for taking such long breaks.

Aaaaand that was one of the most clumsy excuses for a fight scene I've seen in a while.

Ky just told Jo that he nearly left her to die...not sure whether to take that as a warning or expectation of gratitude.

"The caverns! Where you live on Earth!"
"I live in London!"
Well Jo, you could tell him about the Tube.

Wow. I've seen the Doctor use guns before, but this is the first time I've seen him actually fire a warning shot at one of the good guys.

Does it make anyone else REALLY uncomfortable that the one black guy in the cast is called Cotton?

(The moment I learned that Britain sided with the Confederacy during the Civil War because of the cotton industry was a very dark moment.)

How have I gone this far without appreciating Three's scarf in this story?

Oh wow. The design crew for this story apparently had the foresight to include proto-touchscreens. Unless those were already a thing...

Jaeger, I know your name means "hunter," but that still doesn't mean you should attempt justifying genocide in front of Three.

Whew. Good to know that Three won't be operating under a lie told to him by the Marshal for the rest of the story.

On that note, thank you Cotton for being a cool dude and telling him the truth.

So it would seem that the next step is: blow shit up and hope for the best.

Stubbs, you'll forgive me for saying so, but I sense that asking Varan to "just trust you" at this point is quite a lot to ask of him.

Props to Jaeger's actor for getting his face right up in a prop that was about to explode.

I can tell the studio set is still partially lit, but I'm surprised this station doesn't have emergency lights flashing right now.

Varan jumps out and puts Three in a stranglehold, who reacts with a perfect "come on, really? We're doing this again?" face.

The Third Doctor: if he can't convince you with words, he can convince you with two fingers strategically placed at your throat.

"You have no mask. When the sun rises, you will not be able to breathe the air on Solos. No Earth man can!"
"Did I say I was an Earth man?"

Looks like there aren't so much "firestorms" as "fireworks." A bit too colorful.

We finally have our first good look at one of the titular Mutants. Honestly, I can't say these are some of the worse costumes on the show.

That was nice. I off-handedly turned on the InfoText to see if this was location shooting, and the first note to come up was the location.

Hey Ky, remember how just a minute ago you said they were "harmless?" The running away and waving fire around doesn't seem to support that.

Wait, why is Varan talking in third person all of a sudden?

Seems like the mutants are listening to Three but not to Ky. And Jo, if you'd just stayed there a few seconds longer, he might've found you.

Woooaaaaaah are we in the trippy disco cave now?

Oh wait, never mind, this is the Really Shitty CSO Cave.

Although that is most certainly a Disco Hazmat Suit.

Finally the egg reaches its owner. Although I don't think Three needed to dramatically pause THAT long before saying "and to give you this."

Swiggity swegg, what's in the egg? #idontevenknowwhatthatmemeisfrom

Tablets! And one of the symbols on them answers my "what's that shape on the wall over there" question.

"Well what does it say? Read it!"
"I cannot! It is the language of the Old Ones. No one remembers."
WELL. THAT'S. JUST. FANTASTIC.

So Ky JUST HAPPENS to now remember one person who might remember the old language. Chekhov's linguist?

And now: Global Warning with Professor Jaeger.

Oh wow, I think that's the first time we've seen blue sky this whole serial.

Suddenly, from location to studio footage in the same scene.

There you are, Jo! So I wonder when we're going to find out who Disco Hazmat Suit Guy was.

That's an awful lot of smoke...also, ACTING.

Wait hold on is someone talking to Varan telepathically or is he just tripping out.

"Gas. It's the Marshal's solution to what he called the Mutt Problem."
OH HI HITLER ALLEGORY.

Disco Hazmat Suit Guy to the rescue!

Cotton keeps calling Stubbs "Stubbsy." Aww. #bros

Oh, come on Three, don't you know it's not polite to scratch at your host's door like that?

And Disco Hazmat Suit Guy removes his helmet to reveal: dude who was mentioned in passing earlier as the one guy who knew the old language.

Another German, too! Hello, Dr. Sondergaard. (or, wait, is that a Scandinavian name?)

"Marshal, this is not a war! This is a scientific application of ballistics!" #yousureaboutthat

I love how when Ky leans over to look at the tablets, he hugs and strokes the egg for no real reason. #myprecious

("Notice the picture distortion in these shots?") Yes, actually, I did. Why exactly are they necessary in an otherwise normal scene?

Apparently it's to "sell the idea that the mountain is becoming unstable." Um...no.

I think it was the combination of the shadows and red and white light, but for some reason I REALLY liked that last shot of Jo.

Wow, Three, that's easily the biggest ring I've ever seen someone wear on their pinky.

Guys, please stop that distortion thing, especially if you're only using it for one angle on one set.

Wow, I paused on a good face.

Walk into radiation like what up I'm not a human. (This seems to be a bit of a motif in this story.)

Woah. Seems like Cotton's a bit of an acrobat.

And now we return to Varan and his army of Centurion Viking Samurai.

Okay really, is the CSO really necessary for this scene? Couldn't they just make the walls sparkly?

"It's magnificent. It's like a cathedral!" A Sparkly Radioactive Disco Cathedral.

"You go! Leave me!" This should not be as hilarious as it is.

oh my god the music is not helping

We seem to be heading rapidly towards a preemptive '70s sci-fi homage to Indiana Jones, if the jewel-taking and rumbling is any indication.

Guess not, no giant boulder. But he does sling Sondergaard over his shoulder and carry him out like a hunk of fresh game.

Earth inspector is paying a surprise visit and the Marshal is not happy. Slimeballs reacting to incoming comeuppances is always fun.

"Yes of course. The Solonians are *meant* to mutate! The mutation is part of it, part of their evolution." Wow. Can't say I expected that.

With Sondergaard's native get-up, I honestly keep forgetting he's not actually a Solonian himself.

Oh wow. I have to admit, with the countdown and the increasing tempo of the music, this scene is getting impressively tense.

Although that shootout scene was super weak and Varan are you even trying.

And now part of the super-thin hull of the ship is gone and he's floating out into CSO space and WOW THIS SCENE IS SO BEAU-TIFULLY BAD.

I'm still eagerly waiting for the Marshal to lose his grip though. (Seri-ously that is the thinnest goddamn spaceship hull I have EVER seen.)

Oh my god, these poor actors are trying so hard to make the vacuum of space effect look realistic...

Well, it looks like Three and Sondergaard made it out oka*BANG* ...welp I spoke too soon.

The Marshal isn't so much hanging on for dear life as he is slowly humping the wall. (Okay I promise I'll stop taking cracks at this scene.)

wait how did the marshal get out he was just about to die a second ago

Oh hey, firing squad. Usually we don't see you around unless it's a cliffhanger.

Ah, thank you for that perfectly-timed entrance, Jaeger. Ready to punch some Kaijus? (Yup, finally saw Pacific Rim.)

"As for this display of megalomania, how do you hope to conceal it from the investigator?" Jaeger has the sassiest goddamn pose right now.

I love how even though Jo, Ky, Stubbs, and Cotton are all tied up, they have complete confidence in their ability to call the Marshal out.

Oh wow, they have him cornered at every turn. Are you sure we still have a whole episode and a half left to go?

So I'd been wondering for a while who Ky reminded me of, and I just remembered: he looks a lot like Varsh as an adult (if he'd grown up).

Jaeger whose side are you even on anymore make up your miiiiiind...

runs into guard *performs time-fu* "Goodbye!" *runs*

Anyone else find it a little silly that the transporter devices are basically revolving doors? Like...the entire thing is a revolving door?

I really don't know how the guards missed Three just now, considering he's literally black-on-white in this environment.

I think Three just officially ran out of fucks to give. He finds Jo, gets caught, loses the sonic, and he just goes "well what do you want?"

His face says it all, too. I'm surprised he didn't heave a big sigh as well.

"Marshal...you are quite mad." HE LITERALLY DIDN'T EVEN BLINK OH MY GOD

And then we cut to hello Flying Space Toothbrush.

Ah, that's right, this is a great time for Jo's escapology skills to come in handy. The guard's getting sleepy and everything.

BAM. (Seriously, if you don't like Jo Grant, I don't like you.)

And just after they finally get through to the main ship and tell them what's happening, poor Stubbs gets shot in the butt.

wait how did stubbs even die from an ass-shot (also, can we appreciate that pan across Cotton's rage-face?)

And can the guards REALLY not hear the loud gunfire coming from the corridors just outside?

Welp, that escape plan didn't work.

So according to Three, if something went wrong at this point, "we'd all become un-people, un-doing un-things un-together! Fascinating."

Aww, Sondergaard's mutant babbies are all gathering around to protect Daddy from the mean old Overlord guards. I hope.

Well apparently they can talk now. Okay.

The investigator shuttle is about to dock, Jo looks happier than ever, but there's still one more episode so one more thing has to go wrong.

One More Thing That Goes Wrong: Jo, Ky, and Cotton are in a chamber that's about to be flooded with radiation.

"You are a doctor, I take it?"
"I am, yes."
"Qualified in...?"
"Practically everything."

And now we return to your Phallic Imagery of the Evening.

You'll forgive me for not quite understanding how climbing into the refueling tube is going to save them from the radiation.

Oh hey, more oddly-placed CSO.

Huh. That escape plan worked surprisingly well.

JUSTICE WILL BE SERVED. And Sondergaard, I'm not sure bringing the mutants onboard Skybase is such a good idea.

Three finally got the Marshal to crack in front of the investigator. #disgonbgud

Apparently the mutants are intelligent enough to operate the teleporter. Somehow I don't see this ending well...

Yikes, that ended even worse than I was expecting it to.

RAAAAINBOOOOOWS

I rather hope Ky lives through the end of the story. He's been through enough at this point.

OKAY HE DIDN'T JUST MUTATE HE ASCENDED TO ANGELIC HOMOSEXUAL.

I'M NOT EVEN KIDDING HE IS LITERALLY GLOWING WITH RAINBOWS RIGHT NOW.

Fly away, magical rainbow man. Fly away and be free.

AND NOW HE'S JUST GLIDING DOWN THE HALLWAYS AND CAUSING ALL TO FALL BACK IN AWE OH MY GOD THIS IS THE BEST ENDING

AND ALL HE HAD TO DO TO KILL THE MARSHAL WAS RAISE HIS HANDS SLIGHTLY AND VAPORIZE WITH A RAINBOW BEAM

Yay, Cotton survived the whole story and gets a promotion at the end! Good show, ol' chap.

"Doctor...who, did you say?" #yousaidthething

"Back to the broom cupboard." See you next time in Atlantis, guys!

Originally Posted August 2nd, 2013

THE TIME MONSTER

Written by Robert Sloman and Barry Letts
Aired: May 20 – June 24, 1972

Volcanic eruptions...okay show, you have my attention.

and then Three wakes up within the dream to a giant master laughing at him okay how can people hate this serial with an opening like this

"A real pippin of a dream!" And Jo even brought him a cup of tea. #cuties

Anyone else feel like Jo's outfit here compliments Bessie in a way? Probably all the yellow.

"Look, I know I'm exceedingly dim, but would you mind explaining?" Oh. Oh Jo, honey, please give yourself more credit than that D:

Also, hello Master! What's the betting your Alias of the Week is Greek for "master?" Also, nice lab coat.

Your accent, though.

Huh. Is Yates left-handed? Because he's wearing his watch on his right wrist.

Atlantis? Atlantis!

"Against what exactly am I supposed to be warning the world?"
"The Master. I've just seen him."

"Seen him where? When?"
"...In a dream."

I'm betting the Brig is going to be in full "Doctor can we not" mode for the rest of this episode.

Likewise, I may be in "please for the love of god don't make any bad TOMTIT jokes" mode for the rest of this entire serial.

So, from what I gather, the TOMTIT is like a prototype for the T-mat systems in the Troughton serials...so why can't they just call it that?

"Well SOMEone's got to come!"
incoming Benton

Okay, guess I don't need to make fun of the name TOMTIT, the serial is already doing it for me.

Incidentally, I sense an oncoming You Will Obey Me.

Ah, I guess we're going for "you must BELIEVE me" this time.

Oh wait, never mind, we get both.

So we have a male and female scientist talking about feminism, when suddenly the dude turns around and says "Let's do it." #reallybro

"I've asked you a million times, what IS it?" Oh god, that's the Pre-posterously Phallic Master-Detector, isn't it?

"Why the ffffFOOLS!" The way Delgado was holding that F, I coulda sworn he was going to say something a lot more...colorful.

EXCUSE ME WHILE I LAUGH FOREVER AT THAT RANDOM GUY AT THE WINDOW SPONTANEOUSLY DECIDING TO JUMP OFF THE LADDER FOR NO APPARENT REASON

and then it turned into a musical for about five seconds with dancing and WE'VE DONE IT WE'VE DONE IT WE'VE DONE IT and what even

By the way, I'm really liking Dr. Ingram. She's almost like Liz Shaw's younger sister.

"You were drawing power from somewhere OUTSIDE of time itself!" Clearly. CLEARLY.

Also, Mr. Hyde is the most 70s person in this serial so far. He's got the collar, the hair, and the 'stache.

okay has no one seriously noticed the probably-dead body just hanging out in the middle of the parking lot

cue a brief chorus of He Is Not Yet Dead

"It's a doomy old day. I mean, just look at that sky, just look at it!" Jo. Jo you're in England. Jo pls.

Three just flipped a switch on Bessie that was literally labeled "super drive" and all that was missing was Yakkity Sax. #cruisecontrol

Can we just talk for a second about how adorable Benton is when he's like "look sir I figured out the science!"

Well, if we hadn't gone into "I reject your physics and substitute my own" territory before, we certainly have now.

That's a rather nice teacup, why would you want to experiment on that?

When you start yelling "COME, KRONOS, COME!" in the middle of doing a science, you've probably blown most of your cover.

Three to the rescue, in slowwwww moootionnnnn...

A man just aged about 55 years and you want to take him to the hospital? Somehow I think this is beyond your puny human science.

Greek for "master," to the surprise of exactly no one.

"Kronos...yes of course...I should've known..." Is it just me, or is the Doctor being even more cryptic in this story than usual?

"I said, bring some men with you. I feel as naked as a baby in its bath." ...Brig, please never say that again.

On the other hand, what I wouldn't give to have your confidence in speech when taking over a situation.

Aww, Three goes to check on the lab and Benton mentions he's been lonely :(

"The Crystal of Kronos." I'm going to have a hard time keeping my mind in the direction of science and not magic in this story.

Three's referencing going "outside of spacetime" and I can't help thinking that he's referring to the events of The Mind Robber.

Especially since he's talking about having been there before and that it has "creatures beyond your wildest imagination."

Although, everyone from the Land of Fiction was LITERALLY from humanity's wildest imaginations so...maybe I was wrong.

MOTHAFUCKIN CHRONOVORES

"Are you trying to tell us that the Classical gods are real?"
"Well...yes and no."
#percyjackson

On today's episode of Oh That's Where That Gif Came From, Classy Delgado!Master Puffing His Cigar.

I kinda love just how willing Dr. Ingram is to go along with Three's stories. Ancient Greek gods in my science? Okay, sure.

Hey Benton, could you go in and touch that dangerous glowing rock for us? K thx. #whywouldyoudothat

"Do you know why you can't shift it? Because that crystal isn't really here at all." are you completely serious right now

Dr. Ingram isn't even blinking oh my god

Wait, are we in flashback mode now?

On a completely unrelated note, it was interesting hearing Benton say "yeah."

"Doc, am I really an old man?" No, you just have prosthetics on your face.

Granted, it's a pretty good makeup job when the camera's not zoomed in for tight shots.

Wait, can Benton seriously not hear the Master hissing over the director's shoulder to "just do as I say?"

oh nO THE MASTER'S GOING TO DO THE PHONE THING AGAIN

Okay they clearly dubbed Nicholas Courtney's voice over this but sinCE WHEN CAN THE MASTER DO VOICE MIMICRY LIKE THIS I MEAN

For a few seconds, I was sure that Benton was readying for a running jump out the window.

Oh. Actually I wasn't that far off. Benton, I really don't know why anyone calls you dim.

"Nothing can stop me now!"
"...Put your hands in the air."
Where's the Mission Impossible music when I need it.

Also, I love how honestly impressed the Master looks.

"DOCTOR! What a very...*knocks Benton into the lockers* You're wrong, Sergeant Benton, THAT is the oldest trick in the book!" did yOU JUST

A new challenger appears. Greetings, dude from Atlantis!

So the Master went through all that trouble to bring an Atlantian up and his first thought seems to be "shit did I summon the wrong dude."

Master you literally just met this guy why are you offering him part of the universe

Huh. The markings on the Seal of the High Priest look kinda like a precursor to circular Gallifreyan.

"FEMALES, UNDER COVER!" brig no

kronos is here and jesus fucking christ this is one of the most beautifully terrible scenes I've ever seen on this show

"You stay in your kennel till I have need of you!" the master summoned a giant paper-bird-god-of-time and just decided to put it away how

Also, nobody in the cast is very good at running in real time pretending to be slow motion. Not even Nick Courtney.

he's not even really runniNG HE'S JUST JOGGING IN PLACE REALLY SLOWLY HELP THIS IS BEAUTIFUL

"It's safe to go in now, most noble high priest." Yes now that I've put the GOD OF TIME ITSELF INTO A CRYSTAL we can go back in this room.

"I am not slave that I should serve you! I serve only the gods!"
"You will serve me, Krasis, AND YOU'LL LIKE IT."

Krasis, I don't care how confident you are in the defenses around the rest of the crystal, you DON'T TELL THE BAD GUY WHERE IT IS. RULE #1.

Now this is interesting. The temple looks like a studio-bound set, but the video quality is clearly film. Where did they go to shoot this?

why is everyone keeping gods as pets in this story

Oh hey, Stuart's back to normal!

"This isn't a picnic! One minute you're talking about the entire universe blowing up, the next you're going on about TEA!"

Huh, looks like Three got his fill of sandwiches from The Sea Devils. He was just handed a plate of them and turned it down.

Not sure how he's going to delay the Master with a wine bottle and cork, unless he's going to offer him a congratulatory glass of burgundy.

Wait now he's sticking forks in the cork and OH WAIT I RECOGNIZE THIS THING.

"But there's nothing to be afraid of! Do as I tell you!" Yeah, Krasis, give the guy a hand lifting that GOD IN A BOX.

I will probably never get tired of the Brig's "Doctor, can we please not" face.

Did Jo just say "what's up?" She's actually one of the last companions I'd expect to use that phrase.

The Time Monster

"It's just like jamming a radio signal, Jo. We used to make them at school to spoil each other's time experiments." Brig, still unimpressed.

FOOF "...Well, it was fun while it lasted." Jesus Christ I'm not going to miss that noise it was making.

"Images that move and speak!" That's a good question, Krasis: since when has the Master had a CCTV wristwatch?

Suddenly, knighttime.

"Greyhound Three? We're stuck in the mud. Pushed off the road by some goon in fancy dress...I think. Over."
"...Are you suffering from hallucinations, Captain Yates, or have you been drinking? Over."
"I could do with one, I don't mind telling you."

And then, "Another hallucination, sir. Roundheads attacking us with full ammunition. Cannonballs, in fact."

I absolutely love how Yates sounds so nonchalant about this. Like, yup, just another day on the job. Welp.

"Cheers, see you there. Try not to be too far behind." Please tell me this is going where I think it's going.

Called it. #superdriveforcruisecontrol

ALSO THAT WAS THE BEST WHIZZING-GRENADE SOUND EFFECT I HAVE EVER HEARD. AND BY BEST I MEAN FUNNIEST BECAUSE WAS THAT A SLIDE WHISTLE.

I'll bet anything the Master just summoned a bomber jet.

AND NOW THE BRIG IS SAYING "WHAT'S UP."

Yup, it's a V-1 bomber jet. Interesting that Three referred to World War II as "the Hitler War."

WAIT. I FORGOT THAT THE V-1'S WERE THE ACTUAL BOMBS AND NOT THE JETS. So THAT'S why when the engines cut out...

"Yates...Yates can you hear me? Yates, can you hear me? CAN YOU

HEAR ME? OVER. MIKE, CAN YOU HEAR ME?"
#nonononono D:

I mean I know Yates lives, but this feels like the first time the Brig
gets frantic enough that he calls an officer by his first name.

So, not only was that a relatively small explosion, but I'm not even
sure that anyone died?

Oh god, Yates is actually bloodied up pretty bad. (By this show's
standards, anyway.)

And on that note, the Great Master-tracking Phallus is back.

Guys I really love Ingram and Stuart they're so great oh my god.

Ah yes, the infamous Salad Bowl console room.

I think Three's finally figured out that telling Jo to stay put is not a
thing that ever works, ever.

"The TARDIS looks different!"
"Just a spot of redecoration, that's all."
please change it back the salad bowls are undignified

And of COURSE there's a perfectly-sized slot on the console for
Three to stick the base of the penis detector.

"You still want to come?"
"Tis my job, 'member?"
"Glad to have you aboard, Miss Grant!"
"Glad to be aboard, Doctor!"

guys help that out-sweeted the freaking haribo gummies I'm eating
right now

"It always seems to take a long time, but that depends upon the
mood, I suppose."
"What, your mood?"
"No, no, hers. No, the TARDIS's!"
"You talk as if she was alive!"
"Well it depends what you mean by 'alive,' isn't it? Take old Bessie for
instance."
#help #adorablest

Once again, I'm pretty sure the design of the time vortex changes with each opening sequence.

...Huh. Looks like Logopolis is happening about nine seasons early.

"My TARDIS is inside the Master's."
"Yes, but his is inside yours."
"Of course, they're both inside each other."
Of course. Clearly.

I'm quickly gaining more appreciation for the Brig in slow-mo. Because reasons.

"They won't stop me now!"
casually strolls in through the door "Sorry professor, but that's where you're wrong!"
"Ah, my devoted assistants. And are YOU going to stop me?"
"Not by ourselves, no. Take a look behind you."
"...oh come on, REALLY?"

I actually can't with this scene you guys this is so perfect oh my god

"I think I've bruised my tailbone."
"Sorry about your coccyx, Jo, but these little things are said to try us."
#sorryaboutyourcoccyxjo

"I'm sorry about your coccyx, too, Miss Grant!"

Uh oh, looks like turning that thing off didn't unfreeze the Brig and his squadron after all.

PLINGE

Ingram just fiddled with TOMTIT with this big confident grin and told Benton to "just stand there and look pretty." Seriously, I love her.

BENTON MOVE YOUR HAND OH GOD

Welp, the Brig's group is still stuck. Also, BABY BENTON!

("Accurate 'backwards' lines were scripted, but Jon Pertwee chose to talk spectacular gibberish instead.") #ohmygod #ofcoursehedid

also Jo has the best face right now

Oh man, the second Kronos comes out, Three immediately goes into "I HAVE MADE A HUGE MISTAKE" mode.

ALSO CAN WE TALK ABOUT THE FACT THAT THE MASTER LOOKED AND SOUNDED GENUINELY WORRIED WHEN HE HEARD JO CRYING

"But that's the most cruel...the most wicked thing I ever heard!" "Thank you, my dear!"

The TARDIS is broadcasting Three's subconscious thoughts to Jo? Now that's not very considerate of her, is it?

Oh hi Three, welcome back. #wellthatwaseasy

I can't stop laughing at this Atlantis scene and I don't know why?!? Also, hello Ingrid Pitt!

("Cat-lovers may wish to take this rare opportunity to admire the Queen's pussy.") INFOTEXT DID YOU SERIOUSLY FUCKING JUST

Complaints to the king about "superstition and old wives tales" in Atlantis? ...Didn't we already do this in The Underwater Menace?

Ingrid that's not how you hold a cat...okay, that's better.

The Master and the king have only spoken two lines to each other and they're already embroiled in a fierce battle of sass and eyebrows.

Oh, never mind, that ended quickly.

It is possible to give someone a "dat ass" look from the front? Because I'm pretty sure that's what the Master and Ingrid Pitt just did.

So the king might actually be cool after all? Because he just hand-waved the Master's hypnosis and stuck a verbal "fail" sticker on him.

AND THEN HE ASKED THE MASTER WHAT POSEIDON HAD FOR BREAKFAST AND IF ZEUS AND HERA HAD ANY NEW GOSSIP. #atlantiansmackdown

The king told the Master that he wouldn't give him the crystal and the Master just stormed off like a kid who didn't get dessert oh my god

sudden Three "Can't think of anything to say?"
"How about, 'curses, foiled again'?"
do you ever just want to cry because jo grant

IT EVEN HAD A WAH-WAH-WAH-WAAAHHH MUSICAL
CUE RIGHT AFTER IT OH MY GOD

"Strangers are uncommon in our land. Who are you?"
"Oh, this is Jo, Jo Grant, your majesty."
"You are welcome, Jojo Grant!"

An Atlantian king just called one of his subjects "rednecked." Huh.
That's a new one.

Okay, the Master has the bearing of a god. We get it.

Given the way Queen Galleia reacted to Jo's entrance, I wonder if
she's as enamored by Jo as she is by the Master.

So I'm honestly not sure if that Greek cityscape in the background
of the king's chambers are meant to be wall art or an actual backdrop.

guys there is so much sexual tension in this episode I think I'm going
to combust

"What a groovy dress!" Jo where did the rest of that hair come from?

"Look, I'll be as quiet as a...do they have mice in Atlantis?"
"Yes."
"Well, that's what I'll be as quiet as: an Atlantian mouse."

Huh, I didn't know Ingrid Pitt was Polish...

("Because her mother was Jewish, part of her childhood was spent in
a Nazi concentration camp.") ...okay this suddenly got very dark.

Ah yes, sounds like we have an incoming minotaur.

Whoops, looks like Jo's stuck in the labyrinth.

Wow. That's actually a MUCH better-looking minotaur than the Nimon (then again, it's not that hard to look better than the Nimon).

Okay, sure, it still looks like a guy with a head on, but it's a much
better-looking head.

Your daily reminder that Jon Pertwee is a huge trident-snapping badass.

This is feeling very Curse of Peladon all of a sudden.

Although I wasn't expecting Three to go all Venusian Matador on the minotaur.

"He saved my life!"
"I'm afraid he's dead, Jo."
...but you haven't checked. Even though he DID get thrown through a mirror.

Okay, so the cityscape in the background IS actually meant to be the city. Because there's a sunset...underwater...?

The Master tried to pull a "you must obey me" on Galleia and she basically responded with a G-rated "fuck you, no." I think I love her.

"The point is, that day was not only my blackest, it was also my best." YES WE'VE FINALLY MADE IT TO THIS SPEECH.

Wow. Okay, I was going to quote the whole speech but it's about three times longer than I was expecting it to be.

Yikes, that went from adorable to horrifying REALLY fast. That's no way to treat a king, guys. Jeez.

He looks like he's dying but they really didn't hit him that hard...?

The king is dead. Long live the Mast...NO DON'T DO THAT.

Welp, Galleia's only just finding out that the Master duped her and killed her husband. Good timing, since we only have ten minutes left.

She actually tried to hit him! Aaaand then set the guards on him when that didn't work. oH HI KRONOS WELCOME BACK

wait the palace is starting to crash down and now the master is carrying off jo what is even

WAIT HOW IS EVERYONE IN THE ROOM SUDDENLY DEAD

"Just think of the future: dominion over all time and all space. ABSOLUTE POWER FOREVER." No but seriously, I really REALLY love the Master.

Can I just appreciate how cool it is that this basically comes down to a game of temporal Chicken?

"GOODBYE, DOCTOR!" AND CAN WE JUST TALK ABOUT THE FACT THAT JO WAS COMPLETELY WILLING TO DIE TO SAVE THE UNIVERSE BECAUSE OH MY GOD

"Jo...you alright?"
"Fine! Dead, of course, but I'm fine."
............how

wait why did the sky just turn into a giant face HOLD UP IS THAT...

"I am Kronos." YUP. SO THAT HAPPENED.

"And what about the Master?"
"He stays."
"And what will happen to him?"
"Torment, of course!"
#disgonbgud

Aaaaand the Master rushes out and literally begs Three for mercy on his knees. That's...really sad.

...did he just cop a feel on Jo before making a break for it.

Meanwhile back at the lab...

Aww, Stuart is trying to feed Baby Benton. Although I do have to wonder where they found that diaper on such short notice.

Oh hey, the Brig and his crew are finally moving again! Although the smoking TOMTIT doesn't look like a good sign.

Can we just give a round of applause for Nicholas Courtney existing because

HELLO NAKED BENTON (oh bless John Levene's heart you can tell he's trying so hard not to laugh)

("For this bit, John Levene wore an adult-sized nappy fixed with a giant safety pin.") goodnight friends I am gone

Originally Posted November 3rd, 2013

THE THREE DOCTORS

Written by Bob Baker and Dave Martin
Aired: December 30, 1972 – January 20, 1973

Ah, you must be Jo Grant!

And the TARDIS is just sitting abandoned in the background. Poor thing...

HOLY SHIT THAT THING HAS A FACE

It ate the Whomobile...IT ATE THE WHOMOBILE...*

WAIT PLEASE TELL ME THAT'S THE SONIC SCREW-DRIVER

Oh my god it's Gallifrey where did that come from I didn't know the Doctor kept in touch with the Time Lords I thought they exiled him what

TWO! YOU'RE IN COLOR!

So Two and Three are fighting, prompting the crew on Gallifrey to send in One to break them up. Guys have I mentioned that I love this show?

Oh god. I just realized. Eleven has basically the same outfit as Two, just with a different color scheme.

Suspenders, bowtie, jacket, THINK ABOUT IT.

"That's why it's being left up to me and me and me." Patrick Troughton = love.

Wait, TWO had Jelly Babies too? You learn something new every day, I guess...

Hi Omega. Would you mind taking that GIANT helmet off so we can take you some slight modicum of seriously?

"You mean we're not even in the same country?" Poor Brigadier. I don't think his mind is quite up to handling this craziness.

So you're saying that time travel is solar-powered? ......Okay, whatever you say, Doctors.

I KNEW IT IT WAS THE SONIC SCREWDRIVER

GUYS. LISTEN. SLOW-MOTION TIME-FU. THIS IS THE BEST THING.

FINALLY taking the mask off...

OH. MY. GOD. WHAT.

"You're talking about one of the most powerful blokes in the cosmos!" Only Two...

"Oh no, not my recorder!"
"I'll get you another one!"
But seriously, since when did Two have a recorder? I probably missed that one...

THREE IS FREE TO TRAVEL THE UNIVERSE AGAIN!

Also, Omega is probably one of the most wonderfully camp things to ever happen ever.

*I was not aware at the time of viewing that Bessie and the Whomobile were two difference vehicles. The car here is actually Bessie, not the Whomobile.

Originally Posted February 3rd, 2010

CARNIVAL OF MONSTERS

Written by Robert Holmes
Aired January 27 – February 17, 1973

What are those shiny packages? What are those people wearing? Why are the Doctor and Jo on a boat? (ON A BOAT) Someone explain things please

WHAT THE BALLS THAT'S A SEA MONSTER OH MY GOD WHAT

"Allow me, Doctor." *pulls out a crapton of keys* oh my god Jo that was actually really creepy.

THERE IS A GIANT HAND PICKING UP THE TARDIS. JAW. DROPPING. REALLY FAST.

HAH! Tiny TARDIS model! That's actually quite hilarious.

Okay, so they MENTIONED the Daleks...will we actually get to SEEM THEM? Because my Classic Who ventures so far have been sadly Dalek-less.

TIME-FU. PLEASE TELL ME THIS BOUT OF FISTICUFFS WILL RESULT IN TIME-FU.

Correct me if I'm wrong, but the Doctor never PUNCHED ANY-ONE OUT in the new series, right? Except for Eleven in the season 5 trailer?

I wonder how much thought they put into that input/output room. Because it looks like just a jumble of sciencey shapes to me.

WOAH WAIT THEY'VE GOT A CYBERMAN IN THERE WHERE DID THAT COME FROM

MAGICAL ENLARGING TARDIS

So I think the Doctor just used his sonic screwdriver to set a swamp on fire and roast some giant alien worms. This. Show.

HOLD ON, SINCE WHEN DOES THE SONIC SCREW-DRIVER RUN ON GAS?

Oh, real smart, guys. You keep humans in captivity (ON A BOAT) where there just happens to be DYNAMITE.

DOCTOR'S FREE AT LAST!

Originally Posted March 12th, 2010

FRONTIER IN SPACE

Written by Malcolm Hulke
Aired February 24 – March 31, 1973

Interesting fashion choice of doughnut leg-warmers...for your forearms...

Also, how is it so easy for them to move their seatbelts around those Mega Shoulder-Pads?

Cargo ship in pre-war time making a hyperspace jump. Counting down Something Going Wrong in three...oh wait, speaking of Three..

Huh, I wasn't expecting our heroes to be The Thing That Goes Wrong. OH RIGHT. This is season ten so Three can actually fly the TARDIS again!

"Only YOU could manage to have a traffic accident in space!" Hello Jo! Not enjoying TARDIS travel too much, are we?

Woah woah wait...did that other ship outside just...explode and then un-explode?

"A moment ago, it seemed to change shape! It was when I heard that noise...didn't you hear it?" Sorry, Jo, neither did I.

Oh wait, there it is. Also, #ITSATRAP

WOAH SUDDENLY EVERYONE IS TRIPPING BALLS JO RE-LAX THAT'S NOT A DRASHIG IT'S JUST A MAN WITH TWO GUNS

Sir, I understand you need to multitask right now, but I think the point of holding someone at gunpoint is to actually be *watching* them.

Meanwhile on Earth, That '70s Future.

"The treaty between our two empires established a frontier in space." #yousaidthething

On that note, nice to see that Earth has a female president!

With all these illusions and insistence that no one is antagonizing the other, I'm assuming there's a third party futzing around with them.

Also, I wonder why Jo mentioning "bolts" was all Three needed to dissuade him from trying the sonic on the cell door.

"That sound made you see what you fear most." #TheMoreYouKnow

"Seems to act like a post-hyptnotic command." *raises hand and bounces in chair* OOO OOO OOO I BET I KNOW WHO THE THIRD PARTY IS.

"It's only a load of flour!"
"IT'S MY CARGO!"
Huh, we're halfway through this episode and I don't think we know the pilots' names yet.

Wait, who are these guys trying to burn through that door?

"I'm reversing the polarity of my ultrasonic screwdriver's power source." It's...ultrasonic now?

cell door opens *escape interrupted by pilot with gun*
"...oh how very embarrassing good afternoon." *goes back in cell*

Ogrons??!? DID THREE JUST GET SHOT?????!?

This general seems weirdly insistent that everyone on the cargo ship is going to die...insistent in a "just as I planned it" kind of way...

They put Jo back in the cell but they just left Three on the floor? Now that wasn't very considerate of them.

"Doctor...they also took the TARDIS." #wellshit

So we've had the return of the Ogrons and a mention of Solos from The Mutants? Sounds like Three had some nice continuity going here.

"Come on, Jo, let's go and find the crew." *cut to dead-looking crew*

Never mind, they're both knocked out like Three.

Speaking of Three, he's wearing that green ensemble I love so much.

...and under those frilly Victorian sleeves, he has a distinctly '70s wristwatch. Somehow that just makes me smile.

OH MY GOD WHAT IS THE RESCUE TEAM EVEN WEAR- ING YOU GUYS AREN'T PLAYING IN THE NFL IN SPACE #mostepicshoulderpads

"They're traitors!" *guns raised* Huh, they usually don't use these misunderstandings as the cliffhanger.

There sure is a lot of putting Three and Jo back in that cell in this story, isn't there?

I just realized: if this is a cargo ship, would they really have need for a cell? Oh wait...unless they had pirates or something.

Or, in this case, repeatedly-wrongly-accused stowaways.

omg Jo...she sounded so confident coming up with an escape plan all on her own only to learn that the point was entirely moot.

"Hey I've got a TERRIFIC idea! I saw this film once, you see..." I saw this film once #Isawthisfilmonce #joyoureadorable

"JO! Will you stop pacing up and down like a perishing panda!" JO IS A PANDA. Also, come on Three, be a little nicer to the lady.

Sounding more and more like I was right about that third party.

"All we've got to do is find out what's going on, who's behind the Ogrons, where they've taken the TARDIS, go and get it back, and then we can all go home. Right?"
"Right."
"Oh...I don't know what I've been worrying about. :/ "

I know this is odd but...does this story make Jo the first companion to wear jeans? Because I don't think anyone earlier wore them.

Seems like everyone before had skirts, slacks, or suits. Or a kilt.

Anyone else find it super suspicious that General Williams can't seem to look the president in the face for this entire scene? #thirdparty?

...I should really start keeping track of how often Three and Jo get put in a cell in this story because this is...what, the fourth time?

At least the security officers have the courtesy to ask them if they're hungry first.

"Sooner or later, you're going to tell them...everything. They'll use the mind probe." #NONOTTHEMINDPROBE

Aww, Three's being nice to Jo again. "Now come and sit down, stop worrying. Come on, sit down." *hand-hold* #cuties

And now it's time for Storytime with Uncle Three! Today's story: Uncle Three and the Mean Old Medusiods!

"I was on my way to meet a giant rabbit, a pink elephant, and a purple horse with yellow spots." There's a Dr. Seuss pun in here somewhere.

Welp, looks like Three's plea of "let me explain you a thing" didn't work. And is that the first time we've seen Williams smile?

HEY KIDS GUESS WHAT WE'RE GOING BACK IN A CELL

alarm "...Yes well I think we'll sit here for a while after all." Only Three and Jo could make giving up on a prison break look adorable.

Can I just say I love those giant emeralds the Draconians are rocking? I dunno, there's just something neat about large jewels.

Also, I love how they have certain verbal tics instead of sounding alien solely by speaking more formally. They hold their S's a lot.

Uh oh, sniper rifle...SHOTS FIRED. SHOTS FIRED.

Aw, for a second I honestly thought Jo had made a quick escape even in those heels.

General Williams is going to be the better-intentioned Benik of this story, isn't he? They even look kinda similar.

Although, I feel somehow less inclined to punch Williams in the face.

Both sides think Three and Jo are agents of the other side and wow Three is already looking so done.

"General Williams hates our people! Once before, he caused war between us and the Earth men. Now he plans to do so again!" OKAY THIS IS NEW

Ah, time for some Time-Fu! and three just backflips out of the chair in the most beautifully pathetic way possible oh my god I love you

like he didn't so much "backflip" as he did "lean back in the chair really hard and roll out onto the floor"

Actually I take that back: that was still pretty badass.

HEY THERE CELL FANCY RUNNING INTO YOU AGAIN

I kinda love how both Three and Jo have gone from being worried about the situation to being exasperated by it.

Uh oh, there's that hallucinogenic whine again...MORE OGRONS.

Wow, I feel pretty bad for that poor door.

Wait, are the Ogrons busting them out?

"That was close..." *captured again*

Woah, archive footage of actual riots. According to the InfoText, it's the Tokyo student riots of 1969.

"Those two traitors are back in their cell and that's where they'll stay!" AGAIN???

"If you're not seen to act decisively against the Draconians, you can... and WILL...be replaced."
"By you, perhaps?"
#dundunDUUUN

Mind probe time? Mind probe time!

Wow, Three doesn't even look frustrated, he just looks bored. 300% done.

Umm, Williams maybe if you actually turned around and looked at the screen you'd see the Ogrons that Three's talking about.

Aww, Three looks so pleased with himself that he blew up the machine with his mind. #POWEROFTRUTH

Oh hey, it's the cell again. Um, look cell, don't take this the wrong way but...I really think we should start seeing other rooms.

"I like the new outfit. Who're you fighting tonight?" Jo does look like she's on her way to a fancy dress martial arts tournament.

But seriously, could you imagine Jo having a practice sparring match with Three in that outfit? I suddenly want this to happen.

"Under the powers vested in me by the Special Security Act, I'm sending you to the Lunar Penal Colony." DEAD LEAVES!

(No but really, if you've never seen Dead Leaves, you should. It's fun and wacky and original. And takes place in a prison on the moon.)

Meanwhile on the Moon...

That was fast. Also, can we talk about the suspiciously coffin-shaped doors for a second?

Hah! I love how all the other prisoners are still in their blue prison suits and Three just swaggers in like Green Velvet King.

"What did they get you for?"
"...It's a long story."

AND I LOVE HOW THE FIRST THING THREE SAYS TO THE GUARDS IS A REPRIMAND FOR TAKING THAT GUY'S CHOCOLATE

I like this rebel chocolate guy already. I hope we get to learn his name soon.

Woah, hold up...where did these surprisingly fleshed-out criminal records for Three and Jo come from?

"Send in the commissioner from Sirius 4, please." OKAY I'M GONNA TAKE A WILD STAB AND GUESS WHO'S COMING IN NEXT

I WAS RIGHT. Hello Master! Good to see you again! You wouldn't mind helping break Three and Miss Grant out of prison, would you?

Ahhh, so THAT'S what three-dimensional chess looks like!

"There are books, video films, handicraft and discussion groups, all sorts of ways of passing the time."
"Including planning to escape?"
"...That's not one of the things we discuss."

Time for our Daily Appreciation of Roger Delgado's Eyebrows.

On today's Lunar Penal Colony menu: that blue Star Wars milk.

Jeez, have they seriously not given Jo anything to do but just sit and be bored in that cell? Don't worry, you've got a visitor now.

"You...! What are you doing here?"
"To coin a phrase, I've come to take you away from all this."
#helloimthemasterimheretorescueyou

THIRD PARTY IDENTIFIED. #guesswhoitwas

Oh my sweet baby Jo, you've come such a long way since Terror of the Autons.

The Master seems to've reached the point of "dammit Miss Grant you and the Doctor are going to be rescued by me AND LIKE IT."

"ANYWHERE is better than here!" AND MAY THIS BE THE LAST WE SEE OF A CELL IN THIS STORY.

Yay, we finally have someone who believes Three's story!

AND HE'S IN LEAGUE WITH THE GUARD AND THEY'RE BOTH PLANNING AN ESCAPE THIS IS EVEN BETTER

"Come on, professor, come on...you were giving off conspiracy in waves over there." omg Three sounds like a schoolgirl hungry for gossip :D

I find it sort of hilarious that the special sign for the Peace Party is literally just throwing an exaggerated peace sign at each other.

Either that or everyone who's done it so far has really long fingers.

"All we have to do is walk across the moon's surface, ten minutes, and we're there." All we have to do is walk across the moon's surface.

Uh oh...that doesn't look like the trusting glance of a co-conspirator to me...

Oxygen tanks are empty, and I bet that knob was set to depressurize the airlock...I sense a cliffhanger...

Yup and yup!

Three doesn't seem to be banging on the door that hard. Then again, that's probably Pertwee trying not to break the set.

Hmm, now there's a suspiciously familiar black gloved hand...

"I do hope that you're alright, Doctor." Current mood: Delgado!Master saving Three from near-death experiences and asking if he's okay.

Meanie governor, poor Master just wants his Threesies back.

"Some very awkward questions could be asked."
"I have nothing to fear."
You might want to look the Master in the face when you say that.

Also, I love that in a scene with two bad guys, one of them being the Master, it's actually the other guy doing the literal beard-stroking.

can we talk about three's prison gel sandals because

also the fact that his "list of crimes" is basically punching a cop, stealing a ship, and...tax evasion.

Oh and also he apparently robbed a bank, that too.

WELL WHADADYA KNOW. IT'S. ANOTHER. GODDAMN CELL.

Actually, this one's less like a cell and more like a zoo cage. And I was just listening to a Short Trip today with Three at the zoo.

Well, at least Three and Jo are back together again.

"Your health is very precious to me...for the moment." Careful, Master, your sensitive side is showing again.

Wait, I think that cockpit set is a re-skin of the first one or the exact same set. Budgeting!

And now it's time for NUMBERS! Buckle up for safety after doing math!

("This really is the lunar surface, taken from an Apollo landing module.") Oh wow. There's authenticity and there's THE ACTUAL MOON.

"They found me guilty, changed my appearance and exiled me to Earth."
"And that's where you met me."
"That's right, that's where I met you."
"And that alone made the exile worthwhile, Miss Grant."
"Thank you!"
#PRECIOUSBABBIES

But really, Three? Have you seriously never gotten around to telling Jo the story of how you wound up on Earth before?

Good ol' Master, always armed with appropriate reading material: War of the Worlds.

"But if we do get back, I really think you ought to be a bit more reasonable with the Master. I mean, he keeps offering you a share in the galaxy, or whatever's going on, and you keep refusing and playing dirty tricks on him." OR WHATEVER'S GOING ON

Wow, I'm surprised the Master picked Jo's monologue about Three being nicer to him to reach over and turn the volume down.

No but seriously can we just give a round of applause for Jo Grant existing?

BECAUSE APPARENTLY SHE HAS TO GIVE A CONTINU-
OUS SPEECH WHILE THREE GOES ON A FREAKING
SPACE WALK OH MY GOD JO YOU TREASURE

AND NOW THREE'S DOING THE VENT-YOUR-OXYGEN-

IN-SPACE-TO-PROPEL-YOURSELF-BACK-TO-THE-SHIP
THING BECAUSE THRUSTERS

Wait...Master I thought you said you needed Three in good health...
where are you going with that gun?

On the off chance that Three ISN'T floating aimlessly in space
thousands of miles away...

Oh no the Master's making a random offer for Jo on the assumption
that he's on the flight deck aND HE ISN'T WHERE'D HE GO

AH, there he is! Nice fabric-slapping work, by the way.

Don't worry, Jo, the Draconians just docked so you won't have to
worry about the airlock...wait why are they pointing guns at you.

"All diplomatic relations have been severed. You have violated
Draconian space! The penalty is death!" Well...that's inconvenient.

WELP BACK IN THE CELL. Cell, are you stalking us? This is starting to get kinda creepy.

"This won't be my first visit to Draconia, you know. Many years ago I
spent quite some time there." And you wait until now to bring this up?

I love how Three and Jo are just chilling on the bed and the Master's
just standing there doing his best Grumpy Cat.

Oh wait, never mind, he's going down for a nap...and taking out what
looks suspiciously like a distress beacon?

Looks like Ogron reinforcements are on their way.

"Hadn't we better wake our cellmate?"
"He's awake already! He's just trying to show us how unconcerned he is."
evil chuckle

delgado's master is a fucking treasure oh my god

Shoulderpad Game: Draconian Emperor.

Wait, the emperor is actually believing Three's story? This is a
pleasant change of pace.
Usually stories driven by nobody believing the protagonists' truths
drive me crazy, but somehow I've been taking it in stride here. Huh.

I just noticed JO'S BOOTS. CAN WE TALK ABOUT THOSE BOOTS.

(no seriously they look like platform Converses but the camera's too far out to tell)

"I have devoted my life to the cause of law and order and law and order can only exist in a time of peace!"
"You feeling alright, old chap?"

That sound again...OGRON ATTACK!

and the emperor just sits there and watches omg

aHA! Someone finally got to see the hypnosis wear off! #thetruth-willberevealed

YOU get a mind probe! And YOU get a mind probe! EVERY RACE GETS A MIND PROBE!

"The Ogrons've got the finest defense mechanism of all: stupidity. They haven't got a mind for you to probe."

Well, at least the Draconians let up on the misogyny a bit to "respect the customs of our guests" when Jo has something relevant to say.

Hello again, cell! Nice to see you've moved on and let someone else in.

"You know, I think it's about time women's lib was brought to Draconia." Jo, my queen.

Umm...your majesty...that rattling sound behind you is the Ogron trying to break out of the cell...your majesty...?

Oh wait, maybe that's the prince on the flight deck. Either way, looks like we've got company.

"That must be them. No other ship would be on a course for Earth at a time like this."
"WE'RE on a course for Earth!"
"WELL *NATURALLY* BECAUSE WE'RE CHASING THEM!!!!!"

#andersonturnaround #youreloweringtheiqofthewholestreet
Pros of hiring idiots to do your dirty work: they'll do whatever you tell them. Cons: they're idiots.

"You do not wish to kill him?"
"Of COURSE I do! I dunno...rocket fire at long range, it's...I dunno, somehow it lacks that personal touch."

Can we talk about how genius it was that his eyes were in shadow the whole time so it was impossible to read what he was really thinking?

Honestly I have no idea if that was intentional or not, but the effect was fantastic.

Wait...does Three seriously not suspect that that's the Master's ship following them? Or that that's HIS VOICE ON THE SPEAKER?

Okay, granted there's a lot of audio distortion, but I would've thought Three would know the Master's voice pretty well by now.

Ohhhh okay, he DOES suspect something and that's why he's luring them closer to check. That works.

ZEN FIRE ZE MISSILES

Good thing that tussle with the Ogron on the flight deck didn't take too long. On the other hand, Impending Boarding.

And now another episode of The Doctor Would Never Use a Gun, My Ass. (Although I do appreciate that they limit his use considerably.)

(I'm in the "the Doctor can use weapons in extreme circumstances, but he shouldn't make it a habit" school of thought.)

"What is happening? They should have taken that ship by now! God, must I do everything myself?!?" At this rate, Master, you probably should.

On the other hand, they just successfully made off with Jo, so...score one for the Ogrons, unfortunately.

Three and the prince seem to have a lot of trouble standing up, but the camera isn't doing anything weird so...what exactly is going on?

turn on InfoText Ah, the air was escaping through the airlock. But...wouldn't that be pulling them towards it and not pushing them away?

InfoText topic turns to Roger Delgado's untimely death oh no here come the sads

("He didn't turn up for work on the morning of Monday 18 June.")
#no #nononono

("His body was later found in the wreckage of the hire car which was driving him to the location.") #NONONONO

Which reminds me, I'm still amazed that they never got Anthony Ainley to come back and play the Master in a Big Finish audio.

I mean Geoffrey Beevers is great, but Big Finish started doing Doctor Who in 1999 and Ainley didn't die until 2004.

Plus, all accounts I've heard make no secret of just how much he ADORED playing the Master.

Actually, I can probably just ask: @bigfinish, how come you guys never brought Anthony Ainley back to play the Master in his final years?

Meanwhile back on Earth...

Ah, the details behind that initial spark of war between Earth and Draconia 20 years ago finally comes to light!

Looks like General Williams has nothing left to go on, at last.

"Your highness, please accept my deepest regrets for the wrong I have done your people." 'Bout time, man, 'bout time.

And he's even volunteering to lead the expedition to the Ogron quarry! ...I mean, homeworld!

Oh wow, Roger Delgado really was only about an inch or two taller than Katy Manning.

Well, at least we've got the TARDIS back, in a sense. Thanks for the conveniently dramatic lighting, by the way, Master.

"I know that you will obey me." Wait. Is this...? OH MY GOD YES WE'VE FINALLY MADE IT TO THIS SCENE.
"MARY HAD A LITTLE LAMB HIS FLEECE WAS WHITE AS SNOW AND EVERYWHERE THAT MARY WENT THAT LAMB WAS SURE TO GO. HUMPTY DUMPTY SAT ON A WALL HUMPTY DUMPTY HAD A GREAT FALL..."
"STOP THAT, MISS GRANT!"

"It's a form of self-conditioning: you fill your head with nonsense and then you can't be hypnotized!"
#JOGRANTFORQUEENOFEVERYTHING

"ALRIGHT ALRIGHT alright...I was never very fond of nursery rhymes anyhow." GUYS THE MUSIC EVEN FADES OUT WHEN HE GIVES UP

...Oh. This just means he's going to try the fear-wave box on her now.

Drashigs, Mutants, Sea Devils, and Jo just says no to all of it. #ontheartofbeingaBAMF #withjustyourmind

I love how the Master just sees all this as a minor inconvenience. Huh, Doctor's companions don't fall before me anymore. Oh well...

OH GODDAMMIT CELL, I THOUGHT WE WERE THROUGH. I THOUGHT YOU'D MOVED ON.

Well, at least this time Jo's in one where she can plausibly use the old Dig Your Way Out With a Spoon trick.

"No doubt you're a qualified space engineer too, Doctor?"
"Naturally!"

General Williams, I'm not sure if you're trying to look stressed or devious right now...

Wow, the spoon thing actually worked! #praisebetothepowerofspooning

okay is that a really unfortunate rock formation or is there a painting of a liver-shaped bug monster on the wall

("The script describes the wall painting as 'a vast, dragon-like monster, rearing up for the kill, an Ogron in its claws'.") Ah, okay.

Jo's even managing to get a signal out with the Ogron's coordinates to both sides! Remind me again why anyone calls her a ditz?

"Thank you, Miss Grant. That was the trap." ...Bugger.
Aaand the damaged circuitry on Williams' ship is getting worse...how exactly do they plan to wrap everything up in the next 12 minutes?

ESPECIALLY NOW THAT THE HULL IS LITERALLY SPEWING FIRE NOW

Oh, they landed just fine. Okay.

Ogron ambush! But wait OH GOD THERE'S THAT GIANT BLOB THING

I love how the Ogrons are about a half-foot taller than the Master and outnumber him by So Many, but he can part them like the damn Red Sea.

Another ship's landing? Aren't you guys going to go check it out?

"Unarmed, maybe, but not unaccompanied! I've brought some old friends along to meet you!" MOTHERFUCKIN DALEEEEEEKS

Bit early, though, aren't you? Planet of the Daleks is the next serial... oh right, these two stories make up that Dalek War arc.

This is the only time that the Master and the Daleks team up, isn't it? Unless it happens in the Expanded Universe somewhere.

I remember they were in The Five Doctors together, but that was just one Dalek running around in a hall of mirrors and shooting aimlessly.

Bit eager to get to the exterminating already, eh guys?

I think I've officially reached the point where any Dalek that doesn't sound like @BriggsNicholas sounds inauthentic to me.

("The third Dalek operator is having trouble steering, so Roger Delgado surreptitiously gives him a helping hand.") Aww...

Wait...The Three Doctors was filmed AFTER this? ...Okay...?

No, cell, you can't have custody of the kids.

And of course the Master has just one condition for the Daleks' help: can I rule Earth when you're done? Kthx

Ah little fear-box, you will do OUR work now!

"Right, we'll see who rules the galaxy when this is over...'Do not fail the Daleks' indeed, you stupid tin boxes..."

Current Mood: the Master doing a mocking Dalek impression oh my god that was worth the wait.

("The whole session overran its scheduled 10 P.M. finish by 23 minutes.") Wait...I thought the BBC's power always went out at 10?

Speaking of which, only two minutes left and this story feels NO-WHERE near being done.

ALSO DID THE MASTER JUST SHOOT THREE IN THE HEAD

"Telepathic circuits...sending a message to the Time Lords..." ALSO THAT

Wait, the Daleks here were voiced by Michael Wisher? Okay, never mind, turns out they had Davros' voice after all.

Well. There's cliffhangers, and then there's Cliffhangers. With this strong a narrative link, it almost feels like The Daleks' Master Plan.

OH GOD I JUST REALIZED THAT WAS MY LAST DELGADO!MASTER STORY. Rest in Peace, old chap. The Whoniverse wouldn't be the same without you.

Originally Posted January 30th, 2014

PLANET OF THE DALEKS

Written by Terry Nation
Aired: April 7 – May 12, 1973

"Written by Terry Nation." Ah, good to know we've got the big man on board for this one.

Less than two minutes in and Three's already collapsed. Nice quick work on that bed button, Jo!

Aww, she gives him his cape as a blanket.

And on that note, Somewhat Cryptic Instructions Over a Rather Impressive Shot Up Jon Pertwee's Nose.

Huh, I'm digging the new suit, Jo. Might want to make sure Three isn't having a nightmare, though.

Okay I know Jo just said he was "icy to the touch" but I didn't think actual ice would be making an appearance.

ALSO JO I KNOW YOU'RE HAPPY THAT HE'S OPENED HIS EYES BUT IF HE WAS MAKING THAT FACE AT ME I WOULD BE BACKTRACKING VERY FAST

Ladies and gentlemen, we have reached IRL Terrifying Pertwee.

Checking the scanner...everything's in black and white. Have we traveled back to the Hartnell era?

and okay what is squirting ink at the screen with one of the creepiest squirting sounds I've ever heard

Eww, the local plant life seems pretty rude. Come on, Jo's got a perfectly nice coat, don't go messing it up with your plant spit.

also can we talk about JO'S GLOVES.

Please let this episode be a Jo Grant Solo Adventure, please let this episode be a Jo Grant Solo Adventure.

This planet seems exceptionally green. And not just Middle of the Jungle green, but Rave Party green.

Poor coat, abandoned already.

Wait, Three's up already. Maybe this won't be a Jo Grant Solo Adventure episode after all. Oh well...

This...might not be the best time to take those awesome gloves off, Jo. Somehow I don't think that plant spit goes well with bare skin.

Hang on, that one pilot in the landed ship is covered in cobwebs...but he's still moving slightly?

"Automatic Oxygen Supply Exhausted." Wait, really? You'd think the TARDIS would have some sort of converter for that or something.

Ah, there's the rest of the crew. Honestly not sure if they're clones or twin brothers.

Apparently they're far enough in the future that Earth is just a myth. That's...wow...that's unfortunate.

Now we have a third guy and SERIOUSLY HOW DO THEY ALL LOOK THE SAME. (Or at least they all have the exact same hair.)

Hang on, what's shaking up the entire ship and whY IS THAT GREEN INHALER FLOATING AROUND

Oh come on, invisible breather, now you're just making a mess.

Well, now we know what made those triangular footprints that Jo was following earlier...except not really.

"Cabin Atmosphere Unable to Sustain Life." THREE WAS THIS OXYGEN CRISIS REALLY THE BEST TIME FOR AN OUTFIT CHANGE.

Don't get me wrong, I love the crimson velvet ensemble but...I'd also love for you to be able to...you know...breathe and stuff.

Saved in the nick of time but nearly passed out again. Three, you're really not having a good time of it here so far, are you?

"Where are you from?"
"A planet, many systems from here."
"...Skaro! Yes, of course, you're Thals!"
WAIT HOW DID YOU DO THAT

AND DIRECT CALL-BACKS TO THE VERY FIRST DALEK SERIAL OKAY YOU HAVE MY ATTENTION

Soooo that's what the fungal spray does. Might want to find Jo and get that fixed before she, you know, dies or something.

Amazingly, the effect on Jo's hand still looks better than the bubble-wrap from Ark in Space. #easytargets

Wait a sec...a jungle planet inhabited by invisible creatures...I wonder if this is...

Okay, Spiridon is a different planet. I thought it was the same place from The Daleks' Master Plan, but apparently that was called Mira.

Although considering the similar names and similar biodiversity, it wouldn't surprise me if they were in the same system.

"Liquid color spray." Spray-paint by numbers to reveal...a Dalek!

More Planet of the Daleks sometime in the next hour or so. Anyone got any fun Gally stories?

Alrighty, let's watch some more Daleks.

"I've never come across Daleks that've mastered invisibility before." Let's be real though, invisible Daleks would screw us all over *hard.*

There's a background noise identical to something we kept hearing constantly on Kembal in Daleks' Master Plan...

Makes me wonder if Kembal is in the same system along with Mira.

Jo, sorry but somehow I don't think covering your fungal arm with your coat is going to make things much better.

"Early warning system?" Yikes, wish you'd had that for whatever that big tentacle thing is.

THAT TENTACLE THING THAT SCREAMS OKAY WE'VE GOT SCREAMING PLANTS NOW

"If I have to die, I want it to be for a better reason than providing nourishment for a flesh-eating tentacle!" #illjustleavethishere

No no no Jo this is actually a really good time for you to really stay put because collapsing in the jungle would be rather problematic.

Ah, thank you. Hey there Mr. Spiridon, you might want to leave Jo alone. Unless you have a cure for that deadly fungus, which would be nice.

Aaaand just when I was about to ask if the Spiridons had actually been identified as hostile, one of them tries to break a dude in half.

NO GUYS DON'T GO BACK INTO THE JUNGLE GO INSIDE THE SHIP WHERE JO IS.

"COM-MAND. CEN-TER. OR-DERS. THE CRAFT. IS TO BE. DES-TROYED." Ah yes, that would make the ship a worse place to be right now, wouldn't it?

The Doctor: will literally stand between Dalek laser blasts and his companions in trouble.

I still have trouble wrapping my brain around the fact that Classic Who Daleks had non-lethal beam settings.

That said, considering the ship didn't actually explode or anything, I'd say Jo has a pretty good chance of making it out.

Three and an escort Dalek in a lift. Literally all that's missing from this scene is awkward elevator music.

Hello cell, we meet again. I thought you said you were going into counseling. Back to grovel at my doorstep in the middle of the night?

At least Three has company in there.

"They're used to living close to death." Speaking of which, Three seems to be taking Jo's plight frustratingly well.

"Courage isn't just a matter of not being frightened you know."
"What is it then?"
"It's being afraid and doing what you have to do anyway."

After that little pep talk, time to go pocket-diving! Huh, Three's got the sonic with him, that ought to come in handy soon.

Three found Jo's first recording device...please don't turn this into a preview of the tape player scene from the end of To The Death...

Three's face though...such a perfect mixture of grief and tranquil fury...aaaand cut to Jo resting in the most glam of furs.

Wow, okay, the Spiridons can talk after all. That's handy. Maybe you can tell us what that red stuff is before you feed it to Jo?

Oh, it goes directly on the skin. Thank you, Mr. Spiridon!

Although now it looks like Jo's arm is covered in blood.

Sonic doesn't work. Next challenge: checking out the stuff in your pockets and figuring out how to MacGyver your way around a Dalek.

Hey Thals, this probably isn't the best time to be turning your guns on each other.

I imagine Katy Manning must've had fun carrying this scene of just her talking to a floating bowl.

More Thals! And we finally have a female explorer on board now! Shame about that ship crash, though.

"Well somewhere on this planet there are ten THOUSAND Daleks!"
...OH. YEAH THAT'S A PROBLEM.

nO SERIOUSLY THE THALS ALL HAVE THE SAME HAIR

On a slightly related note, wow I really want one of those Spiridon fur blankets. They're so damn shiny...

"Instead of white-hot lava, this erupts with molten ice!" Wouldn't that be...boiling water?

Okay, I know they just said it's a form of ice "that never gets hard," but still. #SCIENCE!

the spiridons with the furs on are like glam rock yetis oh my god

Special delivery of one Jo in a basket!

("Terry Nation wrote this serial with a broken leg: he heroically continued working at the typewriter with the limb in plaster.")

I'm tempted to make a comment about that not being as bad as a broken arm, but I've broken my ankle before so I know how rough that is.

Riding the spinning Dalek: not as nauseating as the Disneyland teacups, but about a gagillion times more dangerous.

"You know, for a man who abhors violence, I took great satisfaction in doing that." It's okay, Three, we all have our guilty pleasures.

Prisoners' escape has been detected and the Thals in the ice vents are about to get blasted. Hope you're still well-hidden there, Jo.

I have to appreciate any Dalek story that shows them actually using their plungers for pushing buttons and opening doors and stuff.

Three, I'm beginning to think that NOT shouting "BACK!" every time you encounter a Dalek is the preferable course of action right now.

You have reached Level Dalek. Sorry, wrong floor.

"I know it's not the moment to ask how you got in there..." YES EXACTLY SO THREE LET THEM OUT OF THE SHAFT

Whew, okay that worked out. Although I'd like to see how that Dalek fixes the jammed ice shaft.

SPLORT or maybe not

Uh oh, there we go, our first Heroic Sacrifice of the serial.

Aaaaand now we're left to question exactly how the Daleks used their plungers to sort through hidden items on a dead body.

Oh come on Daleks why are you wasting time cutting through the door with that dinky-ass heat saw when you can just blast it or something.

Jo's lasted nearly this whole episode sneaking around without getting caught once. *muffled Metal Gear Solid theme in the distance*

"We're certainly not going to float out of here!"
"That's precisely what we ARE going to do!"
#MORESCIENCE!

Oh wow, that makeshift hot air balloon might actually work. On that note, THREE GET BACK TO YOUR ROPE.

On the other hand, locating a huge underground cavern full of Daleks is still pretty handy.

"There's not enough lift to take all our weight!" Which, unfortunately, is exactly what I suspected was going to happen.

Oh wow, that impromptu hot-air balloon seems to be working after all. Also, everyone has really nice-looking shoes.

There's a "how many Daleks does it take to break down a door?" joke in here somewhere, but I guess it writes itself.

"Any idea how far to the surface?"
"Miles, I should think."
THAT IS ACTUALLY SUPER-HORRIFYING.

Frankly I'm not too keen on dangling above Daleks in a tight vent supported only by plastic, some rope, and a lot of hot air.

And now we move on from Dalek Maneuvering 101: Opening Doors to Dalek Maneuvering 102: Moving Rocks.

FOLLOWED IMMEDIATELY BY JO GRANT IS AWESOME 401: BOMB DISPOSAL.

Although that was a highly inconveniently-timed falling rock. Wake up quickly, Jo!

"Just you hang on tight, we're perfectly safe." Cue shot of an ominous tear developing in the plastic. #dundunduuuun

Antigrav disks, ascension, liftoff...oh lovely, now they're being pursued up a narrow space by *flying Daleks.*

And yes, I know flying Daleks are nothing new to us now, but I imagine that wouldn't be so true when this aired.

Jo...Jo get up...JO GET UP...

Ah, that worked out surprisingly we OH MY GOD JO DIDN'T JUST FIX THE BOMBS SHE BLEW UP THOSE DALEKS

Yikes, looks like the plastic balloon picked the perfect time to break. At least they're back on the surface now.

...Oh. Scratch that, at least the Thals are back on the surface now. Three is still clinging onto the access ladder for dear life.

WOAH GUYS HE NEEDS AN ESCAPE ROPE NOT A NOOSE

Rocks fall, Dalek dies.

THREE AND JO REUNITED AT LAST. Hug time!

"We've got to destroy the Daleks!"
"And how does my being here change that?"
"Because...because I love you!"
Aww, Thal-love. <3

The Daleks' biological weapon appears to be a lot of moldy cheese in a box. That...actually seems just gross enough to work.

Got the whole team back together...and I still can't tell most of the Thals apart :/

On the other hand, awwww Jo teaching them about handshakes :)

Alright gang, time to hang out by some geothermal rocks for the night.

Woah woah woah boys BOYS this is no time to be trying to kill each other, now cut that out.

Aaaand so the resident hothead decides to nab the bombs and go blow up the Daleks by himself. At least he had the courtesy to leave a note.

Ah. Now that's more unblinking glowing eyes in one place than I'm comfortable with.

Only two shots left... (insert Sky Captain and the World of Tomorrow joke here)

NONONO I KNOW THE SPIRIDONS TOOK YOUR FRIEND AND YOUR BOMBS BUT DON'T HIT THEM THEY'RE LIKE BIG PURPLE YETI D:

My weakness for big fluffy things may be my downfall one of these days.

But seriously though, Glam Rock Yetis.

And now we come to the slightly awkward choose-your-definition-of-the-word-torch scene.

In this case, "everybody grab torches" does in fact mean "everybody grab a big flaming stick to ward off the monsters."

Oh neat, the Spiridons have names after all! The one who saved Jo is apparently called Wester. Oddly British for an invisible alien.

"Doctor, what shall we do?"
"Well first of all we've got to stop the Daleks releasing their bacteria. Second we've got to make sure that their army stays inactive, and third, we've got to generally put an end to their chances of invasion of other planets."
"Well how're we going to do all that?"
"......I haven't the faintest idea."
#goodtoknowthen

Oh Daleks, bless you and your inconsistent firepower and aiming abilities.

Looks like their moldy cheese weapon has upgraded to Deadly Lemon-Lime Slushie since we last saw it.

Ah, a quarry. Nice to see you again! And you've even got hot springs! How thoughtful of you.

("Filming wrapped that day at 3:20, with little more than a half an hour to go before sunset.") That sounds nuts...

...although having spent an autumn in the Midlands, I can attest (to my American followers) that it's legit. Never got used to it, though.

(For the benefit of my British followers, us New Yorkers are used to end-of-year sunsets being around 5 PM at the latest.)

("And that's why winter location work just wasn't efficient!") You said it, InfoText.

"AD-VISE. THAT. NO. PRI-SO-NERS. ARE. TO BE TA-KEN. THEY ARE. TO. BE. EX-TER-MIN-A-TED." #TAKENOPRIS-ONERS

"A bit winded?" Jo, I'd think you'd be used to all this running by now. Then again, you WERE just outrunning a patrol of Daleks.

("Prepare to see the second Dalek hit the rock as it enters. Rather lightweight for a rock, isn't it?") Sassy InfoText is the best InfoText.

("The two Daleks used on location were not BBC property.") ...How?

Ah, they were made by a separate effects company, that's how.

"AS-SIST!! AS-ASIST!!!" Daleks sounding honestly panicked give me joy in a way I can't quite describe.

As does watching Three and a Thal attempting to *pick it up and drag it around.*

Death by ice-bath. Huh, can't say I've seen a Dalek killed that way before.

Oh...oh no, please don't tell me Wester's a traitor, I liked him!

ON ANOTHER NOTE CAN WE PLEASE TAKE A MOMENT TO APPRECIATE JON PERTWEE IN A SPIRIDON COAT. OR MANY MOMENTS.

"Well Jo, do I pass?"
"You'll do, in a pinch."
#cuties

Oh my god. Wester wasn't a traitor...actually, I think he just saved the whole world at the cost of his own life.

Rest well, Wester. You were a noble soul. A shame we get to see your face only in death.

Uh oh, apparently a single glimpse of boot was all that Dalek needed to blow our heroes' cover.

Hey Daleks, suggestion: if you want your vision to be impaired less often, maybe you should have more than one eyestalk or something.

...said the human who only has one vision center that can't be much larger than a Dalek eyestalk and no laser gun to discourage attackers.

(To clarify, yes I do have full use of both my eyes, but humans don't have eyes in the back of our heads any more than Daleks do.)

That was an odd tangent...anyway, back to giggling at the Thals trying to run under the cover of the Spiridon glam rock coats.

My heart is seriously sinking into my chair at the prospect of Rebec getting burned alive inside that Dalek casing just now.

"Well Rebec, it seems you stopped being a Dalek just in time." Whew!

Incoming ship...and it looks like...ah, I bet that's Dalek Supreme. Looks good in gold.

Wow. Round of applause to Terry Nation for such a great dual-sided analysis of how hope can mean the difference between success and failure.

It cracks me up how Daleks "trying to break in" is literally just them ramming against the door repeatedly.

This is the first time in a good while that I've seen a Dalek go full-on "YOU HAVE FUCKED UP NOW" on another Dalek.

Uh-oh, the Daleks have started to move! *insert MGS alert signal here*

Also, war flashbacks to Licegate 2013.

...Dare I ask why you put the bomb right on an open ledge?

On the other hand, Three climbing into a nest of half-awake Daleks is pretty damn ballsy.

Aaaand boom goes the Dalekmite.

The group's back together, the bomb is set...but there's still about 10 minutes left, so there's time for one more thing to go wrong.

Somehow I sense a Heroic Sacrifice coming up in the next few minutes or so.

Since I feel obligated to comment on this, no it doesn't bother me that the hibernation chamber is full of toy Daleks and not "real" ones.

Frankly, they achieve the sense of scale well enough for me. Their movement is a little jerky, but not a real problem.

"...It failed." ...Okay, I'll admit I didn't see that coming.

Oh wait, never mind, here we go. ICE VOLCANO TO THE RESCUE!

"When you get back to Skaro, you'll all be national heroes. Everybody'll want to hear about your adventures."
"Of course!"
"So be careful how you tell that story, will you? Don't glamorize it. Don't make war sound like an exciting and thrilling game."

Oh Jo, the next time an adventurous young man asks you to go with him is going to come along much sooner than you think. And you'll say yes.

(Guess who still hasn't quite processed that The Green Death is the next story?)

INCOMING DALEKS. And amazingly they made it back inside the TARDIS just fine, despite the acid plants and the crust all over the doors.

"WE. HAVE. BEEN. DE-LAYED. NOT DE-FEAT-ED. THE DA-LEKS. ARE. NE-VER. DE-FEAT-ED."

"But Jo, that's only one little world! There's so many hundreds of others to see!"

"There's only one little world I want to see right now."

THAT WAS IT. THAT WAS THE LINE. THAT WAS THE THING I SAW IN THAT ONE CLIP AND KEPT WAITING FOR IT TO COME UP AND NOW IT'S HERE WHEN I'M DONE

"That one."

"That one? But Jo, that's Earth."

"That's right, Doctor. Home."

"...Home it is, Miss Grant :)"

excuse me while I feels everywhere

guys I just finished up all of jo grant's serials what do I do now #help

Originally Posted March 21st, 2014

THE GREEN DEATH

Written by Robert Sloman and Barry Letts
Aired May 19 – June 23, 1973

Okay, time for The Green Death, my last Instant-Pertwee arc. *sigh*
Again, I miss him already.

Wait a sec, this seems to take place immediately after The Three
Doctors, because they're talking about the TARDIS working properly
again...

Also, the audio is slightly out of synch. Crap.

Never mind, working again.

If it wasn't for the age difference, I'd say Three and Jo made a cute
couple. Also, synch problem seems to be recurring but fixable-ish...

"This fellow's bright-green, apparently. And dead." I really like the
Brigadier.

"Jo, you've got all the time in the world. And all the space." Listen to
him, Jo. THIS IS THE WHOLE POINT OF THE SERIES.

Also, might not keep up a commentary this time. Busy wrestling with
the audio problems.

"So...the fledgling flies the coop..." *gets into TARDIS and leaves*
Aww, poor Three...losing another companion...

So the Doctor goes to a planet of blue things, gets attacked by EVERYTHING EVER, and goes back to Earth to pick up the phone. THIS SHOW.

I'm still trying to figure out Bert. Is he getting sweet on Jo, or is he just a creeper? Also, Doctor in cherrypicker = win, for some reason

YES. MORE TIME-FU. THANK YOU THANK YOU THANK YOU THANK YOU.

"Venusian Aikido, gentlemen. I do hope I haven't hurt you." The Doctor is the best person always forever.

OH SNAP. I think Three's getting jealous of the long-haired hot-shot scientist who's stealing his girl. I mean...companion.

Gradually inching my way along in The Green Death. WOAH THAT GIANT MAGGOT JUST LEAPED UP AND ATTACKED A GUY. JO, PLEASE TURN AROUND.

THE COUNTDOWN. MINE-BLOWING-UP TIEMS NAO.

"Theyre'll be no more of these creepy-crawlies, that's for sure." *everyone stops and stares at Brig* Scientists + soldiers in the same room

Wait why was there a woman in a bathrobe walking around the company base I don't even

AHAHAHAHAHA Three's glasses-and-mustache truck-driver disguise FTW.

Oh wait, even better: MILKMAN!Three. Also, I'm calling it now: the fungus kills the maggots.

"Would you like a nice cup of arsenic?" ...wow, Jo.

OH. OH NO. NO. WHY. WHY ARE YOU SHOWING US PERT-WEE IN DRAG. WE NEED TO SEE THIS EVEN LESS THAN HIM IN THE SHOWER.

Third Doctor dressed as a window-cleaning lady. Will my eyes ever recover?

"...Don't say one word."
"......I like your handbag."

Okay, scene forgiven and redeemed. Also, Yates looked WAY too eager to see Three.

FUNGUS CURE. CALLED IT.

And just when I thought "I am the boss" was going to be followed by "I am the Master"...it wasn't. "I am the computer!"

Finishing Green Death tonight. OH GOD PLEASE DON'T LET JO AND JONES DIE HORRIBLY TOGETHER.

Whew. Okay, they're safe-ish in the cave now.

"The following statement is false. The above statement is true." HOLY SHIT HOW DID I KNOW THE DOCTOR WAS GOING TO DO THAT.

Owned and OWNED.

Mind control does not work on Three! "I'm just doing a few sums to keep myself from getting bored. Now let's see, Pi...3.14..."

Three is making a 70'S COMPUTER mad by effortlessly resisting mind control. That. Is. Amazing.

ESCAPE BY MILK TRUCK. My god, Three is one of the most badass fuckers ever.

Random Yates with gun!

Alien mind-wipe sapphire crystals? Doctor, what DON'T you have?

Last episode of Instant-Pertwee!

So now evil-overlord computers hum to themselves while their minions work? Nice.

1) OH SHIT GIANT FLYING BUGMAGGOTTHING. 2) Just. Feed. Jones. The fungus. YOU'VE ALREADY FIGURED OUT THAT IT'S THE CURE. USE IT.

WOW WHEN DID YATES TAKE THAT MANY LEVELS IN BADASS.

How do you stop a giant mutant bug? By throwing Three's coat on it. BECAUSE HE'S THAT AWESOME.

"We should've arranged for the symphony orchestra to herald my triumph!" 35-ish years later, the Master proves that this would be awesome.

Why are musical bad guys always the BEST. THING. EVER. on this show?

First Oscar Wilde quotes, then classical music, now metaphors. This is quite a cultured evil computer.

D'awwww, Jones is going to live!

All I can think of during this scene is the bit from Spongebob with "LOOK AT IT! LOOK AT IT! LOOK AT IT! I WANT ALL OF YOU TO LOOK AT IT!!!"

So the villain sheds a tear for his computer "friend" and...wow, they're really good at blowing shit up in this arc.

Jo and Jones getting married and then exploring the Amazon? ...wow, I can tell this is a little much for Three to take in at once.

Wait...MARRIED?!? They just met a few episodes ago!

So Three drives off forlornly into the sunset, alone again. Don't worry, Doctor. You get Sarah Jane Smith next!

Originally Posted February 12th, 2010

CHARACTER RETROSPECTIVE: JO GRANT

Once upon a time, I tried to divide up all the female Classic Who companions into several categories for a thesis paper: the Kids, the Screamers (which was admittedly a bit harsh), the Intellectuals, and the Action Girls. But there was one companion that I decided to close the paper with, because she seemed to defy categorization. That lady was one Josephine Grant. Jo is a character that I'm particularly defensive of. My earlier experiences with fandom tended to write her off as a "dumb blonde" or "useless," but my time watching her proved that she was anything but.

Jo is very much a heroine with heart. She's not incompetent or fragile, just flawed in some places and strong in others. She's been shown to both hold her own in a fight and save the day with The Power of Love, but she can get in over her head sometimes. And let's be real: who hasn't? I think her most telling moment comes when she's undoing the Doctor's handcuffs and he asks about her science A-levels. "Didn't say I passed," she replies with a sly smile. Jo is also an expert in not always doing what the Doctor tells her, which tends to work to everyone's advantage. She saves him just as much as he saves her. I have a particular fondness for "The Daemons" for many reasons, but one of them is Jo's tremendous display of self-sacrifice at the end. I frequently judge companions by whether or not I would feel safe traveling with them, and I would gladly travel with Jo Grant anytime. She may not be a brilliant scientist like Liz Shaw, or a battle-hardened warrior like the Brigadier, but she has courage and smarts where it counts.

Having a full three seasons on the show, Jo is offered the great opportunity to unfold and develop over the course of her time with Three and UNIT. For instance, compare her encounters with the Master between their debut in "Terror of the Autons" and the Master's untimely finale in "Frontier in Space." If you listen closely, you'll notice that even the soundtrack falters in her wake. Most of Jo's klutzier moments happen earlier in her run, except for her fumbles in "The Green Death" which still wind up working out for the best. The more we see of Jo, the more we learn about her. We get tidbits about her background, her fears, and her relationships with the other UNIT chaps (I sense that if this era took place in New Who, Jo, Benton, and Yates would have been prime fodder for a love-triangle subplot. Especially after re-watching "The Three Doctors" and listening to the Big Finish audio "The Magician's Oath," which features an older and regretful Yates mourning that he never told Jo he loved her).

Then there's her departure. I'm usually not a fan of companions leaving to be with a man they just met that same story, but I think Jo's was one of the better-handled romance exits. It's clear that Jo has a particularly strong bond with the Third Doctor, so it makes sense that she would fall for someone her own age who reminded her of him. Her scenes with Cliff Jones don't always show off her best side, though. Still, Jo was my very first Classic Who companion departure and, at a point in my viewing when I wasn't sure if Classic Who hit as many emotional notes as New Who did, I was sorry to see her go.

Needless to say, I was super excited when they announced that Jo would be returning for a special *Sarah Jane Adventures* story along with the Eleventh Doctor in 2010. Her camaraderie with Sarah Jane was an absolute joy to watch, especially after they established that the Doctor's perceived favoritism wouldn't be an overriding issue, and it was just so nice to see two women over 40 working together to save the day on a kid's show. It breaks my heart that we'll never get to see that team-up again, at least on TV, but it still makes me happy that the wonderful Jo Grant was able to make such a stellar return.

THE TIME WARRIOR

Written by Robert Holmes
Aired: December 15, 1973 – January 5, 1974

Nice. This is the first time I've seen this intro in context. AND IT'S A ROBERT HOLMES STORY!

Also, I think this is my first Pertwee since The Sea Devils (no, The Five Doctors doesn't count, no matter what @TardisTavernTit says.)

The lowly meal of straggling medieval soldiers is suddenly interrupted by BALLS FROM SPACE.

Once again, I kinda feel like I'm watching a serious episode of Blackadder. I think it's the costuming. And the music, to an extent.

Our first look at a Sontaran! Welcome to Earth! Now please leave.

Also, why are you holding a baseball bat?

Oh. That's not a baseball bat, that's a flagpole. With white flags. And you're conquering. Kinda sending off some mixed signals, Linx.

Also, sorry but I think you landed a few centuries too early for alloys and complex circuitry. A lot few.

Meanwhile, back in the "present day" at UNIT HQ, THREEEEEE! It's been way too long! And BRIG! As an actual Brig!

"All my eggs to one basket, so to speak."

"Well that's fine...*DRAMATIC CLOSE-UP*...so long as no one steals the basket."

Well, I think I've put all the pieces together of why this story is called The Time Warrior in the first place.

Maybe this is just me being really really slow, but I only JUST realized that Three has a bowtie. It blends in with the jacket really well.

"Oh there she is, Miss Smith..." Oh my god there she is.

The one, the only, Sarah. Jane. Smith. Ohhhhhh goodness, what a legacy you've got ahead of you, girl.

(The previous Tweet is quite possibly the greatest understatement I will ever make in one of these commentaries.)

"I thought all this might give me a good story. I'm a journalist. Sarah Jane Smith."

Again, it feels like I've seen so little of Sarah Jane that it's kinda weird seeing her now.

First impressive thing you notice about Sarah Jane: she's enough to hold the Doctor's attention while some random dude paws at the TARDIS.

Okay, so he just draws the line at people...well...drawing their lines on the TARDIS.

"Are you loyal to your lord, boy?" ..."boy?" The man's got a beard! Heck, EVERYONE here seems to have beards.

"A war? That is excellent."
"Ohhhh, so you like war, eh?"
"Who does not?"
#sontaranverbalwin

Wow. Indeed, keep your glasses on. I think that's the only time the Doctor has been mistaken for one of his companions.

Anytime Sarah Jane and Three come in close proximity of each other, the snark levels soar and I think I love it.

Three, you can sleep in ways I simply cannot.

Also, the Doctor's Device of the Day goes whiiiiiir when there's stuff.

Wait, the Brig just said "oh my giddy aunt." I wonder if Two rubbed off on him somehow.

"Brigadier, a straight line may be the shortest distance between two points, but it is by no means the most interesting. Goodbye, old chap."

Huh. I wonder why the "Police Public Call Box" decals on the top are gone this time. Or nearly invisible.

"Well done, old girl. Absolutely on target." *immediate flashback to The Doctor's Wife and "I always loved it when you called me Old Girl."*

A guy who I could swear was Robin Hood tries to assassinate the captain but is interrupted by Sarah Jane asking for a phone. This show.

Well, now Three knows he has an accidental stow-away. Might want to go in and save her. She doesn't look very happy.

And the helmet comes off! Creeeeepy ugly dude.

"Why don't you stop this ridiculous pantomime?!" Should I start counting the minutes before Sarah Jane realizes this isn't a ren faire?

Although, I have to admit her "doesn't take shit from no one" attitude is pretty impressive. But we'll see when she learns the truth...

I'm more amused than I should be at Sarah Jane saying the phrase "buxom serving wenches."

"Girl? You have two species on this planet?" .... #nocomment

Aaaaaaand here we go, Companion's First Hypnosis.

Looks like Linx built a warrior robot. Or something. It's tall and shiny, anyway.

"By heavens, Linx, I never thought when I first saw you that I should come to love you as a brother." Ah, good ol' interspecies bromance.

There we go, Doctor and companion reunited! ...For about three seconds...

I think that's the first time I've ever seen the Doctor pick up a crossbow. Naturally, his target wasn't organic.

And Irongron gets his first look at a Sontaran. Not sure he was quite expecting, well, this.

So I'm assuming Three is getting to experience what medieval "ventilation shafts" were like.

Maybe I've just never noticed it before but...what's that thing he's got danging around his neck? Doesn't look like the TARDIS key...

I'm liking Rubeish more and more. He's certainly taking the whole time-travel (and slavery) thing really well...

Uh oh. Sarah Jane thinks that Three is the one making the "magic weapons" for Irongron's army. This can't end well.

"What is your native planet?"
"Gallifrey. I am a Time Lord."
If I remember right, that was the first time Gallifrey was mentioned by name.

Nice hat, Three. I'm assuming it's going to be about as effective as the mind control device in your last serial.

Jon Pertwee, how have I forgotten how magnificent your face is?

"Will you excuse me? I've got to go and find a young girl..."
"Young girl? Should've thought he was a bit old for that sort of thing."

Suddenly, TIME-FU.

Interesting choice of cinematography. A big wide action scene all shot from one bird's-eye angle.

Wait...I thought Three was holding a spear when he went down in the hay. Did it magically disappear or something?

Well, that's one way to shake off pursuers: set everything behind you on fire. Especially when Everything is straw.

"Is this Doctor a long-shanked rascal with a mighty nose?" Jon Pertwee's Mighty Nose #jonpertweesmightynose

Ah, here we go: Three and Sarah Jane finally get to sort things out with each other. Hopefully. It IS the third episode, after all.

"How do I know you're telling the truth?"
"Because I never lie. Well, hardly ever."
Rule number one...

"My dear girl, I don't go around kidnapping scientists!" A man from Coal Hill School named Ian Chesterton begs to differ.

Okay, I really don't remember Three being this...not sure if "misogynist" or "sexist" fits this situation better...

So I just remembered: Linx is repeatedly described as being short, but he's really only a few inches under most of the rest of the cast.

"MY species? You're talking as if you weren't human!" Times like this I need to actively remind myself how little Sarah Jane knows now.

"You're serious, aren't you?"
"About what I do, yes. Not necessarily the way I do it."
#classiclines

BATTLE IS ABOUT TO COMMENCE.

Well, the dummies have failed thanks to the power of GUNS. Time for Plan B, which I expect will involve Three's s'ploding bags.

Aaaaaaand boom goes the (orange) dynamite.

I think Sontaran makeup is a lot more effective from a distance. Up close, you can see where the mask and the flesh are separate.

On the other hand, I think the same can be said for most Classic monsters.

For some reason, I can't help but notice that the wine in this serial is REALLY red.

Judging by his speech and Bloodaxe's expression, I can't help but wonder if Irongron is getting increasingly drunk off that wine.

Ahhhhh, so THIS is where those images of Three and Sarah Jane in monks' robes come from.

plays that Chanting Monks music from Monty Python and the Holy Grail

That looks like Two's sonic screwdriver, but it isn't. Is that just a pen light?

I think Rubeish is about to inadvertently discover what will become the quintessential means for defeating Sontarans from now on.

Oh. Never mind. He just had it explained to him by Three.

This is something I don't say very often but, if Three took Rubeish to a doctor that fixed his eyes, I'd like to see him become a companion.

You know, I think this is the first time I've heard the Doctor talk about the effect other planets' environments have on their inhabitants.

I mean, think about it: don't the vast majority of alien worlds visited in the Whoniverse have Earth-like or nearly-Earth-like conditions?

Well, either that or the story takes place on a base and if someone goes outside, they die. Or something like that.

We interrupt this mature and adult-like observation to bring you a re-minder that Brits like to pronounce "robot" like "robutt." #iamtwelve

While I usually love the design of historical Who stories, it's driving me nuts how the wooden doors in studio shots are obviously NOT wood.

"THIEF!"
"You...common scullion, stand aside!"
Sarah Jane, I love you.

Oh god, why am I suddenly expecting that Star Trek fight music from Arena to start playing here?

Gender Roles 101: Companions work in the kitchen while the man kicks ass elsewhere. #sigh

"I cannot reveal my face, Irongron."
"Why?"
"Because if I did it might give you a seizure."

Ah. I can see what everyone's been saying about Pertwee-era Sarah Jane being more of a feminist-written-by-men.

This'll be interesting: death by firing squad that doesn't know what guns are.

Even better: escape by swinging chandelier!

Further escape, whistle causally and punch out the guards. Cut to the dinner table.

"Time's beginning to run out..." As indicated by the Big Flashy Lighty Thing.

Now I wonder what this thing is that Three's got out of the TAR-DIS. Looks like window blinds that've been re-purposed into a fan.

Well, that mysterious potion seem to be taking effect. Guards go sleepy time now.

Oh, and Sarah Jane finally gets to wear her original outfit again.

"Now all you have to do is this...this...and this." Jon Pertwee: Master of Technobabble Evasion.

Okay, time for Sontarans vs. Time-Fu.

Two minutes left and things aren't looking very good...

The. best. arrow shot. Holy crap.

Castle goes BOOM. Oh look, there's a conveniently located TAR-DIS.

"You are truly a great magician, Doctor!"
"To tell you the truth, Hal, I'm not a magician at all."
"I'm not so sure about that..."

Aaaaaand we're done! What's left to say but oh, Sarah Sarah Sarah...

In Loving Memory of Elisabeth Sladen

Originally Posted May 25th, 2011

INVASION OF THE DINOSAURS

Written by Malcolm Hulke
Aired: January 12 – February 16, 1974

Ah, the gentle tweeting of birds over a quiet London...a quiet, very empty London...

Unimpressed Sarah Jane is unimpressed.

The Doctor using an actual telephone booth? Now there's something you don't see every day.

Our first civilians! Although I bet that van is full of UNIT men.

"...There's no bus."
"There's no anything. Nothing's moving."
Except that key you've become fond of spinning around, Three.

"Perhaps it's Sunday. Great Britain always closes on Sunday." And after 5 PM.

Wow, that's a lot of litter in the street. A lotta litta, if you will. #sorry

Considering how empty the city is, I'm surprised that apparently only one dude is going around and looting.

Although if we're talking about looting in the '70s, I think New York is the place you'd want to be. Or not want to be.

can we please talk about how sarah jane was perfectly willing to chase down a guy with a gun #bamf

Although I do love that her second reaction is "do the sensible thing and call the police."

woah WOAH IS THAT BLOOD OR DOES THE ROBBER HAVE HALF HIS FACE MISSING

Ah, UNIT HQ at last. Hello Benton, Brig!

"Sir, five more looters have been picked up in Hyde Park." Ah, thank you, Yates. I figured there was more than one.

Wait, *organized gangs* of looters? How long has this been going on??

And I'll bet that's one of them now. Time for some Time-Fu.

This story is actually really dark so far? Or maybe that's because we haven't made it to the beautifully shoddy dinosaurs yet.

...apparently I said the magic word because there's a pterosaur of some sort right now.

Shoo, dactyl, shoo!

(My dinosaur phase was easily about 15 years ago, so I may use a lot of incorrect terminology for the duration of the serial.)

"Waiting for this mysterious scientific adviser of yours to turn up?"
"That's right sir."
"I suppose he'll just materialize out of thin air"
"...Very probably."

Seeing the Brig taking orders instead of giving them is really strange. Then again, he REALLY doesn't want to take THESE orders.

Well, this is certainly a new take on Doctor And Companion Turn Up At The Wrong Place And The Wrong Time And Get Arrested.

"Age?"
"Twenty-three."
SARAH JANE IS MY AGE? AND SHE'S ALREADY SO MUCH COOLER THAN ME.

Aww, Three's having fun with his mugshots.

"Now, what about one of both of us?" no it's too soon after Jo left I can't go calling you "cuties" yet

That was actually quite a nice building explosion. Not so sure about the T-rex, though, if that is a T-rex. Maybe an allosaurus?

I'm not sure who I should be giving a bigger You Tried star to: the production team for the dinosaurs, or the UNIT chaps fighting them.

"Good grief." For those times when you're so shocked that you need to borrow someone else's catchphrase.

There goes Three's classic "if military bureaucracy had a face, I'd punch it" face.

Welp. When the going gets rough, consort with criminals, apparently.

"So much for honor amongst thieves." So that's what happens when you bring an aikido to a gun fight.

can we please talk about jon pertwee's face

Ah, I see they've started calling him "Doctor Who" in the credits instead of "Dr. Who."

Also, aww, that poor t-rex has a broken neck.

Okay, I promise I'll keep the cheep shots at the dinosaurs effects to a minimum from here on out.

Umm...guys, unless you're trying to bring that building down on top of it, might I suggest shooting AT the dinosaur?

("Swinging from Pertwee's neck is a magnifying glass pendant. It was a parting gift from Katy Manning.") BBYS

"BACK! BACK, ACCURSED WIZARD!" ...well, that's one way to make an entrance. Hello there. Why do you look like an adult English Jamie?

"For a moment there, time went backwards!" IRL rewind button.

That one time Three almost chopped the Brig in the face. (Huh, he almost got his wish from earlier.)

"It's a color-code, Doctor. We're using red pins for tyrannosaurus, blue for triceratops, green for the stegosaurus, and pink for your

pterodactyl."
"...Thank you, Benton."

"We therefore evacuated the entire area and set up this temporary HQ, which you can see from the map is on the periphery of the zone."

Actually Brig...from the paintings on the walls, it looks more like an elementary school.

"Who's this?"
"Sir, this is the Doctor, our scientific adviser."
"Ohh, we've been waiting for you, you know. May I ask where you've been?"
"...Certainly."
"...Well?"
"You can ask, but I can't guarantee that you'll get a reply."

I love how Three is easily the tallest person in the room, despite technically being doubly outranked.

"How much do you think we'll learn from a dead dinosaur?" ...quite a lot, actually.

Awww, stegosaurus! Don't shoot it, it's a herbivore! Okay yeah it could mess you up pretty bad with those tail spikes but...herbivore!

Yates seems to've taken to Sarah Jane quite quickly. Probably missing having Jo to talk to. Seems rather happy about London being empty too.

Well, certainly looks like someone has a cosmic remote control with a temporal rewind button around here.

Yup, there's our Mysterious Presumably-Underground Lab.

"Tell you what, I'll fix you up with a temporary pass." I keep forgetting that Sarah Jane doesn't have the same UNIT clearance that Jo did.

On today's episode of Oh So That's Where That Gif Came From: Jon Pertwee's Collapsible Hair.

"Our friend from UNIT is here." Wait...oh no, please don't tell me it's...

YATES NO WHY

On a lighter note, aww, Three finally has an interruption he wants to stop and chat with.

"I'll do nothing to harm the Doctor, nor will I allow him to be harmed!" Whew, at least Yates has some priorities straight.

("John Levene asked Pertwee not to look at him while saying the words 'large, placid, and stupid'.") omg

I wonder if "closing shot of t-rex roaring" was the "closing shot of Colin Baker's horrified face" of this serial.

Three...Three this is not a good time to suddenly be falling over...

Yates to the rescue? Yates to the rescue!

"I agreed to delay his experiments, not to kill him!" Thanks, but if you could explain *how* the module was killing Three, that'd be nice.

That was the most pained "I'll do what I can" I think I've ever heard from someone in Classic Who.

"Mind you, that creature isn't what I wanted at all. What I really wanted was a Brontosaurus."
"What's the difference?"
...brig no

Atta girl, Sarah Jane! See Three, this is why you'll be glad to have an investigative journalist for a companion.

I'll bet anything this Dr. Whitaker is one of the scientists that Yates is working with.

I'm not sure if that look the Brig is giving Sarah Jane is one of admiration or condescension.

Now the question is, is Sarah Jane going to stay behind anyway and catch Yates in the act?

I guess not. But wow, that's an impressive "oh my god why isn't anyone listening to me" face.

Aaaaand just when I thought the general was actually helping her out, he goes and makes that sinister aside to the camera when she leaves.

Okay, Sarah Jane might not just be about to catch Yates up to something, she might even get a photo of it.

Also, her gleeful "yay pictures!" face is completely adorable.

wait WAIT SARAH JANE I THINK THE FLASHES ARE WAKING IT UP

RUN GET OUT OF THERE OH MY GOD YATES PLEASE DON'T TELL ME YOU LOCKED THE DOOR

Whew, Three to the rescue! And I have a sneaking suspicion that that warehouse is about to come crashing down.

Sabotage is duly noted. Now we just to wait and see how long it takes them to solve the mystery.

I love how Benton doesn't even put up much of a protest when Sarah Jane has a plan. Just business as usual by this point.

"Wasn't there a plan once to build underground quarters for the government in the event of an atomic war?"
"Yes, back in the Cold War days!"

Ah, hello UNIT Dating, fancy running into you again.

Interesting how the InfoText gives a brief summary of the Cold War, even though I imagine everyone watching this DVD would know what it was.

"It's right here! It must be under this building!"
"...After you, Miss Smith."
PLOT TWIST #SECRETTUNNEL

Aaaand what's the betting that this room with the weird flashing blue lights is for memory wiping?

OKAY NEVER MIND SHE'S ON A SPACESHIP NOW WHAT?

"We left Earth three months ago!" ...well I can't say I saw this coming.

Ohhhhhhh wait! I'll bet that room was a time machine and Sarah Jane's been thrown into the future.

"Someone attempted to murder Miss Smith by locking her in the hanger with the creature!" Just learning about this now, eh Yates?

Okay seriously who ISN'T in on this Golden Age plot by this point??

"This new car of mine is exactly what I need." omg is that the Whomobile?

Meanwhile, back in space, Sarah Jane...recognizes everyone she's meeting on the ship?

I wonder why Three's clipboard says "Don't Forget" at the top in really faint letters.

Huh. Either Three's a good lockpick even without his sonic, or he inherited Jo's skeleton keys.

And now it's time for a game of Trap the Doctor in the Maze!

"He's in the lift. Is everything ready?" They're not going to try to gas him, are they?

Nahhh, that would be too easy. Let's do it the fun way and pluck a pterodactyl out of time to eat him!

Doctor used Mop! It's not very effective....

"You've got a warped view of things."
"You mustn't say such things!"
"I'll say whatever I like!"

"Re-educated" is never a good word to hear in these stories...

I'll bet Three and the Brig are going to go to the broom cupboard and find it's been switched out somehow.........yep.

Welp, the minister's driver was also the underground scientist the whole time.

"If she doesn't respond to re-education, we'll have to destroy her." We'd really prefer it if you didn't do that.

I think a better title for this serial might be Oh Sure They're Nice Now But You Just Wait.

Well, at least someone in the base appears to agree with Yates' standing on not murdering people.

Yup, one of the scientists is Whitaker! Although I'm surprised he's decided to just call Three directly and introduce himself.

That big humming orb thing certainly isn't suspicious at all, nope.

Oh hey, a stegosaurus! "There's your monster-maker, Brigadier, caught in the act!" ...OH.

"Doctor, you're under arrest." Only two episodes left, so that shouldn't last long.

CAN WE TALK ABOUT HOW SARAH JANE SMITH IS A BADASS

Well, it's good to know the Brig isn't entirely on board with the whole arresting Three business.

"So it was you, Mike."
"I'm sorry, Doctor."
:(

Poor Benton, he knows he's going to come off badly in this so he just gets it overwith right away.

Anyone else getting a City of Death vibe from that localized time control machine?

Meanwhile in space, Mission Impossible theme intensifies.

Sarah Jane, I reeeeaaally wouldn't recommend the pushing of random buttons. Especially in space.

"...Well don't just stand there, Benton, put yourself under arrest!" #briggetsthingsdone

I take back my earlier comment: thank you for pushing those random buttons, Sarah Jane, now that we know they don't actually do anything.

Sarah Jane Smith: ready to risk stepping out into the vacuum of space with no protection to prove a point. Dang, girl.

LIIIIIES, IT'S ALL LIIIIIIEEESSS.

Oooo, is it time for a car chase with the Whomobile?

Wait, of course that's not the Whomobile, it's a UNIT jeep.

Bro, you're on a manhunt, I'm not sure this is the best time for a smoke. On the other hand it'll help Three escape, so please have a smoke.

Whew, at least Sarah Jane made it back to UNIT HQ alright.

Uh oh, counting the minutes before the general turns on her...

gun Ahhh, there we go.

Today's traffic advisory: dinosaurs. Dinosaurs everywhere.

Run, Three! Run while that poor brontosaurus is bleeding...water...?

"You realize this is mutiny?"
"There's no question of mutiny, I'm just doing my job."
Can we please give a round of applause for the Brig?

Three found Sarah Jane's note! It's all coming together now...

"Excuse me sir, but um...are we evacuating or not?"
"No."
"Oh. Well in that case sir, um...what should I do?"
"Oh go and make us all a cup of tea."

YATES NO PUT THE GUN DOWN

Ah, this is your first trip through a ventilation shaft, isn't is, Sarah Jane?

"There's no alternative!"
"Yes there is: take the world that you've got and try and make something of it. It's not too late."

Ah there's our teBENTON TO THE RESCUE

Aww, Brig, don't blow up the stegosaurus, it's friendly!

"Never thought I'd find myself blowing up a Tube station. If you're wrong Doctor I'm going to have a job explaining this to London Transport."
"Well, don't worry, Brigadier, I'm never wrong."

Hey Brig you think you can keep that triceratops busy for me while I rig these explosives k thx

Aww, dino doesn't like the flare.

That sounded like a much bigger explosion for the amount of light it gave off.

Benton's doing a lot of tackling people with guns in this story, isn't he?

"You'll be court-martialed for this, Sergeant!"
"Yes sir! Very sorry sir!"
AND THEY CUT AWAY RIGHT BEFORE HE DECKED FINCH IN THE FACE

(okay, no idea if he actually does or not, but the implication and the hand-raise was pretty heavy)

Sarah Jane's got the people out of the "spaceship," Three's in the base, we've got five minutes to fix everything.

WHITAKER THREW THE SWITCH COME ON THREE TIME TO TIME LORD IT UP IN HERE

"NO, HE'S REVERSED THE POLARITY!" Famous last words.

"It's not the oil and the filth and poisonous chemicals that are the real cause of pollution, Brigadier. It's simply greed." #themessage

So Yates is resigned and off on sick leave? At least he's getting help.

"Still I'll say one thing: not many sergeants get the chance to punch a general on the nose!"
"Just don't make a habit of it, Benton."

Hey Sarah Jane let me tell you about this awesome planet... not listeninnnnngggg Doctor...

Originally Posted May 25th, 2014

DEATH TO THE DALEKS

Written by Terry Nation
Aired: February 23 – March 16, 1974

A refugee fleeing in an acid swamp desert and getting axed by an arrow. Cutting right to the chase, are we?

(We're literally only a minute in)

Hello Three! Don't think I've heard your delightful singing voice in a while.

That's quite an impressively colorful inflated waterfowl you guys've got there. Off to a day at the beach?

The TARDIS doesn't sound too healthy. Waiting for something about the mercury fluid links any second now...

Or maybe not. Although apparently the lights in the TARDIS were keeping everyone's voices from echoing this whole time.

"Hooray for old-fashioned oil!" Ah, the power of analog lighting.

Mysterious new planet! Let's take a look around...Sarah Jane, you might want to put on something warmer than a swimsuit.

Atta girl. Three...Three is this really the best time to be wandering off? Usually that's your companions' job.

Those beings in cloaks are decidedly less glam than the ones from the last Dalek story.

Also it looks like they weren't stone after all.

Easy escape for Three. Good thing he doesn't have to deal with guns. Yet.

No Sarah Jane, don't go to the light! ...wait...wow, actually yes please go to that light.

Meanwhile, back in The Quarry...

Ah, finally other people! This was turning into a surprisingly dialogue-lite story for a bit.

It's The Future And We Have Archers!

"Are you from Earth?"
"...In a roundabout sort of way, yes."

Forbidden City? ...oh, maybe going towards the light wasn't such a good idea after all.

Certain death? Somehow I think it'll take more than Death by Smothering to keep Sarah Jane down.

Oh. I was ready for the Rare Substance of the Week to be something used for deadly weapons or Mad Science.

"I think we can safely assume that no help is coming. So! Might I make a suggest..."
"THE RELIEF SHIP IT'S HERE C'MON QUICKLY!!!"

Hey there did someone order a shipment of DALEKS?

"TO-TAL EX-TER-MIN-A-TION. FI-RE. FIRE!" Huh. Good thing their guns seem to've taken the day off.

"Well well well. Daleks without the power to kill. How does it feel?"
"KEEP A-WAY. KEEP A-WAY."

Considering Pertwee apparently wasn't too fond of the Daleks, this scene must've been rather satisfying.

Meanwhile back at the sacrifice chamber, or I'm Surprised This Wasn't The Cliffhanger...

Collaborating with Daleks? This'll be interesting.

...Okay, how is it only JUST occurring to me that they're fighting with archery because their guns won't work in the power outage?

Well, this is certainly a very different kind of shootout from what we're used to seeing on Doctor Who.

Aaaaand boom goes the Dalek.

(Although you'll forgive me for not quite understanding how getting hit with sticks repeatedly causes a Dalek to explode.)

Lucky for Sarah Jane this ceremony is taking so long.

Ah, never mind. Three to the rescue!

Really though, Daleks being de-powered and turning to diplomacy is REALLY satisfying to watch.

Aaaaand of course I say that RIGHT before they finish their improvised weaponry.

Daleks to the res...cue...?

"I think they expect that sacrifice to be completed by something else. Something that lives down this tunnel." Minotaur time?

Actually no, it's Zombie Exxilon time.

So is it just me, or does that tentacle creature kind of look like the aliens from the original War of the Worlds?

Oh hey, the Exxilon zombie is friendly! And he can speak!

"That way leads to death!" Well that's inconvenient.

Hey Mr. Tentacle, think you can blow up that Dalek for us? K thanks.

Ah, Three and Sarah Jane reunited at last. "The root: 1. Dalek: nil."

Worshiping a city as a god? Huh, that's new.

They sure seem to be blowing up a lot of Daleks in this story, don't they?

"I saw them too, Doctor. Do they mean anything to you?" Those markings do look weirdly familiar...

"You see, I've seen them before."
"Seen them before? Where?"
"On the walls of a temple in Peru."
"Oh, that's impossible!"
"That's what they said about the Peruvian temple as well."
#imnotsayingitwasaliens #butitwasaliens

The Incredible Disappearing Doctor and His Exxilon Friend

First stop: Skeleton Exhibition. Next stop: Maze.

Whew, for a minute I thought they were going to have to navigate through an *actual* maze.

Hold up, that pattern on the floor looks familiar...is this...?

Yup, the infamous Worst Cliffhanger.

Look out, Three! It's A PATTERN!

The rules of Venusian Hopscotch appear to be "step on the white panels, not the red."

"Was that really necessary, Doctor?" Don't worry, we were all wondering the same thing.

...Oh. Yeah, I guess that was necessary.

I sense more impending exploding Daleks.

Or not. I guess the Cybermen from The Five Doctors could've learned a thing or two from these Daleks.

Sudden Betrayal Wall!

insert Blinded By the Light joke here

Well, now we've had several glimpses of the Exxilon Behind the Curtain. Maybe this whole city-god thing was rigged by one guy after all?

"Now what?"
"Well, if I'm right, the ultimate test will be an assault on our sanity."
Uh oh...

Oh god, this is a bit more than an "assault on sanity," this is a "give the entire audience one big seizure."

(Seriously though, this episode needs an epilepsy warning.)

Did...did the Exxilon Behind the Curtain just disintegrate for no apparent reason?

"Our entrance must have created a current of air which broke the surface tension." Ah. Thank you, Three.

"FE-MALE HU-MAN HAS E-SCAPED. I HAVE FAILED. FEMALE PRISONER HAS ESCAPED I HAVE FAILED I HAVE FAILED SELF DESTRUCT I HAVE FAILED"

I think this is the first time I've seen a Dalek have an all-out panic attack because of an escaped prisoner.

Three Three THREE TURN AROUND too late.

Oh. I guess the easy way to defeat a Dalek is to A) be immune to their makeshift guns and B) punch them.

Centuries in the future and we'll still have Rolex watches in space.

Four minutes left...somehow I doubt this Dalek capture will last very long.

Come on, Galloway, time to prove you weren't a power-hungry coward this whole time.

Godspeed, sir. You did the right thing.

And down goes the city...with what sounds like the desperate wails of all those Exxilons inside...

"It's rather a pity, in a way. Now the universe is down to 699 wonders."

Originally Posted July 31ˢᵗ, 2014

THE MONSTER OF PELADON

Written by Brian Hayles
Aired: March 23 – April 27, 1974

It was a dark and stormy Peladon night...or day...I can't really tell in this place. Either way, looks like as we left it last time.

Everyone's hairstyles seem to've changed quite a bit, though.

Yikes. Looks like the vengeful spirit of Aggedor doesn't just kill you, it completely disappears you.

ALPHA CENTAURI! Good to see you again!

Ortron...he was the aide from Curse who wasn't Hepesh, right?

"Galaxy 5"...any relation to Galaxy 4?

"The citadel of Peladon, Sarah! One of the most interesting and..."
"...Oh no it isn't."

Seems like nearly every opening so far this season has been the TARDIS landing and Sarah Jane being unimpressed.

Wow. That drill works so well it's messing up the DVD.

Looks like Peladon hasn't abandoned the Roman Centurion look for their guards. Although I don't remember the animal-hide throne plinth...

Okay, I guess Ortron wasn't in Curse, otherwise he should've recognized Three.

But Alpha Centauri does! Aww.

"She is of no importance"? I can feel Sarah Jane's done-ness radiating off the screen.

You know, I had the impression that Queen Thalira was supposed to be kind of a pushover from the "only a girl" scene, but she seems pretty in control so far.

Warring factions, rebelling underlings, audiences with the queen, ambushes...this is starting to feel like a Wayfinder game.

Case on point: only one dude in the room has a sword. Respect his status!

Unless you're the Doctor, then you Time Fu your way out of pretty much anything.

"You see the dangers we face, Doctor? Peladon is still a barbarous and primitive planet!"
"When miners have to take up arms to protect their rights, they probably have their reasons. I'd like to know what those reasons are."

Seems we have a new Champion! Ah, that's right, poor Grun was a casualty of Big Finish.

(and I say that with the utmost respect. I loved Prisoner of Peladon)

"Well, I'll say one thing for your friend the Doctor: he's got quite a knack for talking himself out of trouble."

"Hmm. Just as long as he hasn't talked himself into a whole lot more." #thatsit #thatstheshow

insert Boom Goes the Dynamite joke here

Wow. Poor Champion didn't even survive the first episode.

The Third Doctor: can fight off swarms of guards, but can he dig his way out of a cave-in with his bare hands?
Answer: no. But at least he had help before the spirit of Aggedor came to vaporize him.

Regardless: Sarah Jane, leather jacket on, to the rescue!

"For the good of Peladon. You see, I have a special interest in this planet." I do hope he'll go back there in New Who at some point.

Can't say I was expecting a spearfight here.

Actually wait, it's not spears, it's swords vs. sticks. And rocks.

Wow okay. Sticks and rocks: 1. Swords: 0.

Sarah Jane, I know you're a bit frantic, but sometimes banging on mysterious doors in caves gets you zapped by rainbow waves.

Campfire Story Time with Peladon miners!

Ettis seems to be our main Disgruntled Rebel for this story. What's the betting he'll pull some more sabotage later on to get his way?

"I say we attack again!" Yup, there we go.

"There's nobody in there."
#paynoattentiontothemanbehindthecurtain

Seems Peladon has kept a few trends: dudes in mini-skirts, purple velvet, and royal advisers who are suspicious of All the Things.

"It's no good, Sarah. The only thing these people understand is..."
STAB

Um, Alpha Centauri, I love you but degrading the locals like that is reaaaally not a great idea.

We'll befriend you...befriend you with our SPACE GUNS! (ah, good ol' camp references from 2007)

Manhandling Sarah Jane seems to be a new pastime in this episode.

"I think I could've faced death myself for an honorable cause!" Sorry Alpha Centauri, but somehow I doubt that.

But I will certainly give you credit for bringing Queen Thalira around on the whole saving-Three-and-Sarah-Jane issue.

If Aggedor is still alive and in that cave of punishment...why? Didn't they learn last time that he was basically a giant lap dog?

S'up Aggedor.

"Come on, Aggedor, that's no way to greet an old friend!" I thought so.

Ah yes, time for a rousing round of Venusian lullabies derived from Christmas carols.

(No seriously, listen to Voyage to Venus. It was Pertwee's idea, but Big Finish basically made it canon.)

Well, that solves that problem. And is it just me, or is something smoking just outside the control room?

"What 'advice' did the Doctor mean?"
"Well it's going to be rather difficult to explain, but I think he was referring to Women's Lib."

Odd conclusion to come to, since I don't think we've touched on gender politics at all yet in this story. On the other hand...

"It would be different if I was a man, but I'm only a girl!"
"Now just a minute! There's nothing 'only' about being a girl, your majesty!"

Ah, there WAS something smoking just outside the control room: a torch. Of course.

I was already relatively confident in Thalira's skills of argument, but Sarah Jane's pep talk really seems to've given her a boost.

Gebbek seems to be becoming gradually less moderate as the story progresses. This...could be a problem.

Sarah Jane, I'm not sure if you're proposing to pretend that everything's going fine, or if you're about to solve this whole crisis alone.

"A most excellent scheme, Sarah! Worthy of the Doctor himself!"
Wow, that's quite a high compliment. Wonder what she's got planned...

The sad conclusion of the epic saga of Three and His Glass of Water.

"From here, we dominate the citadel!" *DUN DUN DUUUUUUN*

Wait...I recognize that voice pattern...do we have incoming Ice Warriors?

Oh wow: a rare occurrence of the sonic screwdriver actually being used as a screwdriver.

Ortron actually talking sense and getting people to agree? Well now, Sarah Jane really does have something brilliant cooked up.

WELP THAT WASN'T WHAT I MEANT BY "INCOMING ICE WARRIORS" BUT OKAY

"Do not move! You are my prisoners!" Aww, and I though the Ice Warriors were supposed to be good guys now :(

Although I'll admit, it's kinda fascinating to hear the Ice Lord talking with such a range of intonations.

Need to add more complexity to your miners-vs-politicians plot? Throw in a third party!

My attention is a bit split in this scene: on how Peladon unites against the Federation, and how it looks like Three's hair is on fire.

...wow okay I wasn't expecting them to wipe out all but one miner in one go.

"We will be revenged." I wonder if that means Ortron is going to stop being our token Corrupt Official for this story?

It just occurred to me that we're a full eight minutes into this episode and Sarah Jane is only just now getting a line.

Alpha Centauri is whispering and it's adorable.

I don't think I've ever heard the word "cooperation" used that many times in one speech.

Uh oh, our sole survivor Ettis is back and he's not happy...

"You'll be killing our own people!"
"That's riiiiight! Kill them! Kill them all!"
Ah, so we've reached that point, have we?

It kinda feels like the story is wrapping up, but we've still got two more episodes to go?

Whew, good to know that guy Ettis stabbed lived to warn Gebek about what was going on.

"Look after Sarah for me."
"WHA??"
three no

Umm, guys, you can probably stop hitting that Ice Warrior now. I think he's down.

Also, I think Gebek just pulled an "it's dangerous to go alone, take this."

And I'm glad he did because it's time for a SWORDFIIIIIIGHT.

Commander Azaxyr has really thought this out a lot more thoroughly than I was expecting.

I was about to make a "never bring an aikido hand to a knife fight" joke but then I didn't need to.

OR MAYBE I DID BECAUSE HOW IS ETTIS PUNCHING THE STUFFING OUT OF THREE

An explosion big enough to "kill everyone in the immediate area" apparently means "kills the person operating the switch."

omg poor Eckersley, he just wants to do his job and when Azaxyr tells him to suffocate the miners he just. leaves.

Ah, thank you Gebek, feels like we haven't had a good line fluff in a while.

Oh noooo, how long will Sarah Jane have to think that Three's dead D:

Azaxyr was apparently plotting a full takeover of Peladon the whole time. At this point, I really shouldn't be surprised.

So we've got a human journalist, a queen, a chancellor, and big green phallus teaming up to save the day. This show, you guys.

"Your majesty...do you think you could faint convincingly?" Sarah Jane Smith I love you.

A monarch of Peladon kneels over the fallen body of once-trusted aide turned radical but redeemed in death. And so history repeats itself.

Oh. Forget what I said earlier about "poor Eckersley."

Although I did find it slightly hilarious that he literally has a big red Aggedor button.

Ah good, Sarah Jane knows Three is alive now.

When in doubt, bung a rock at it.

Despite being outed by Alpha Centauri, Eckersley is still being chill as a goddamn cucumber.

If you don't love Queen Thalira at this point, I don't know what to tell you.

Make up your mind, door. Do you have a giant hole melted through you or not?

Also, the Ice Warrior's lips don't seem to move. like...at all.

How have I gone all this time without mentioning Azaxyr's fabulous cape?

Crack the defense mechanism up to RAINBOW LEVELS!

Ah, I'd forgotten that the Ice Warriors are apparently on the Doctor's list of Races He Can Straight Up Murder.

I dunno, maybe it just rubs me a little the wrong way because the Ice Warriors are more humanoid that the Daleks.

How many times has Gebek said "Aggedor fights FOR US!" in the past ten minutes?

"Turn it off!"
"You wouldn't use that."
"Wouldn't I?"
As Snake would say: is this your first time pointing a gun at a person?

"Have a look." Aaaaaand that went exactly where I expected it to.

Usually I don't approve of companions wearing heels, but I'm digging Sarah Jane's boots for some reason.

Ahhh, THERE'S my "never bring a knife to a gunfight" joke!

Azaxyr is finally taken down. Now we just need to take care of Eckersley...

Huh, you'll forgive me for saying so, Sarah Jane, but I didn't know "aw screw it" was a Stage of Grief.

"I shall summon assistance! HEEEELP!!! GUARDS!!!" oh my god alpha centauri I love you

Is it wrong of me that I find Sarah Jane's "HOLY CRAP HE'S ALIVE" face really hilarious?

"Tears? Anyone would think you thought I was dead!" Well, that's totally not an ominous echo of the next serial, that's for sure.

"Come on, quickly!" Didn't...didn't you just go down that tunnel?

Need to track a bad guy through a labyrinth? Just use Aggedor!

oh no nO NO NO YOU DID NOT JUST SHOOT AGGEDOR

Huh, I guess a bear hug from a mythical beast was all it took to save the day. Nice.

"There's nothing 'only' about being a miner, your majesty, anymore than there was about being a girl!"

Doctor, don't grab your companions by the ear, that's rude.

Originally Posted October 6th, 2014

PLANET OF THE SPIDERS

Written by Robert Sloman
Aired: May 4 – June 8, 1974

rings gong SPIDERRRRRRS.
SPIIIIIIIIIIIIIDERRRRRRRRRRRRRRS.

"By Robert Sloman." I have to admit, for a brief second I thought it
said "by Robert Shearman" and I got really excited.

Now who's this taking a leisurely stroll? Wait...is that...? Yates?...
YATES IS THAT YOU??

Cut straight to Three and the Brig listening to some guy making some
really bad jokes about Archimedes being a streaker. We're a minute in.

I have so many questions. Where are they. Why are they watching a
variety show in a tiny room. How did Three talk the Brig into joining
him.

And now we have men sitting and chanting in a basement. If this was
a DVD instead of iTunes, I would have the InfoText on right now.

Ah, so it IS a summoning ritual! I expect it'll be a while before we
find out what that mysterious blue glow was.

"Well, you enjoyed *that*."
"Extraordinary muscular control. Very fit, that girl. I must adapt
some of those movements as exercises for the men."

"It'll take some adapting."
why did it take me so long to come back I've missed this banter

I'VE ALSO MISSED THE BRIG OH MY GOD HIS FACE
WHEN THE PROFESSOR SUGGESTS THAT UNIT DOES
CABARET

Interesting twist: the clairvoyant professor started his mind-reading as
an act but THEN developed actual powers.

Brig a frightened man just made a lunch tray levitate I'm not sure this
is the best time to say "You should use that in your act."

Hi Sarah Jane! Aww, it's nice to see you and Yates getting along so
well again.

Wow, everyone's being a douche to that one guy with the flower. He
just wants to make pretty things and tea...

"It's definitely a job for UNIT."
"Well then you must tell the Brig or the Doctor!"
"Heh, you think they'd believe me? Last time we met, I pulled a gun
on them."
"Ohhhhhhhhh, NOW I get it!"

Unexpected tractor hallucination? Unexpected tractor hallucination.

"This watch was given to you...eleven years ago. You received it...in a
hotel...a hotel by the sea...Brighton, was it? From a young lady...called
Doris. She said it was to mark her gratitude..."
"YES ALL TRUE ABSOLUTELY SPOT-ON."
brig omg

I need to know the rest of this story now holy crap. So the Brig and
Doris have known each other for that long? Nice.

"It translates your thoughts into pictures on this monitor here." The
one invention I'd like to see become reality before I die.

Oh, Three, come on, don't give him your sonic to read, you'll overload
him! Seriously, how many centuries of memories must that thing have?

"And, that's what meditation is all about?"
"Yes! The old man must die, and the new man will discover, to his
inexpressible joy, that he has never existed!"
...Not quite sure I understand that philosophy but okay.

"Doctor, I...ah! Doing a bit of hairdressing on the side, eh?" Hi Benton!

HE HAS A PACKAGE FROM JO!!!

Wait...wait...oh no...ohhhhh nooooo I suddenly have a really bad feeling about what might be in that package...

"From beyond the stars..." PLEASE DON'T TELL ME SHE SENT BACK THE METEBELIS THREE CRYSTAL THAT WAS THEIR PARTING GIFT

Oh...? Three's actually smiling? Whew, okay, I thought he'd be at least a little broken up about it.

Sarah Jane Smith: cannot be kept out of anywhere.

Well this is interesting, she's quite eager to stay a while longer but Yates REALLY wants to get her out of there.

"So why are we running away?"
"We're not. We're letting him THINK we're running away. Now, we'll go back on foot."

Ah, so Jo only sent back the crystal because the South American natives were afraid of it. Good to know.

Hey, the flower-and-tea guy is back! And apparently his name is Tom. Hello Tom! Sorry, Sarah Jane and Yates don't have time for games now.

Sarah Jane, I appreciate your kindness to strangers, but I have a feeling that someone's going to find that pin and wonder where Tom got it.

I'll bet anything that the ritual has something to do with the crystal. Which would explain the psychic wind storm in Three's lab.

"You're too late, Brigadier! He's dead!" Oh. That's unfortunate.

To summon 1x medium-sized alien spider: chant in a circle and accidentally kill a man.

Ohhhh, so these aren't just giant spiders, these are giant ZAPPING spiders!

Giant zapping TALKING spiders!

Also, dude, why are you telling it to leave when you just spent all that time summoning it?

"Are you feeling alright?"
"Of course I am! Never felt better!"
Somehow that always seems to be code for "I've been possessed."

BENTON CALLING HIMSELF "EXPENDABLE" MADE ME A LOT SADDER THAN I WAS EXPECTING

and he looks so sad when Three won't let him risk his life for the team oh my god Benton are you okay

Looks like the spiders want their crystal back. Well, to be fair, I don't think we ever saw the Doctor ask for it.

"Oh, is that you, Sullivan? Get over to the lab straight away!"
Sullivan? WAIT IS THAT HARRY?

"Look, never mind the dratted coffee! What about the spiders?"

Aww, I think Three's going to tell the Brig the daisiest daisy story. If the Brig doesn't cut him off first.

Yikes, Tom was actually threatening to hit Yates if he didn't listen to him.

Can we please talk about Sarah Jane's coat for a second

ALSO IS THAT THE WHOMOBILE I THINK IT IS

"May I see your pass?"
"I CAST PAIN! PAIN TEN!"
(that's what he said right?)

Umm, guys, I recognize that you're having a very important conversation, but now might be a good time to notice the creeper at the window.

Casting Teleport? Well, that's one way to get your stuff back.

Wow, Benton really isn't having an easy time of it in this episode, is he?

...okay I know the joke is that UNIT's bullets never work, but...you can NOT be telling me that the Brigadier is that bad of a shot.
Or maybe moving targets are just that much harder to hit. I don't know, I've never fired a gun and have no plans to.

Chase time! After the stolen Whomobile in Bessie.

For a second I actually thought the license plate on the front of the Whomobile said "NYOOM."

That is literally the tiniest flyable non-toy helicopter I've ever seen.

I imagine that police officer's day is about to get a lot more interesting.

A man possessed by an alien spider just stole a time traveler's hovercraft and now he's about to hijack the world's tiniest helicopter.

Why did it take me so long to get to this serial.

I remember reading somewhere that Jon Pertwee actually drove the Whomobile around on the streets because why not (can someone confirm?)

"Panda Three to Control...you'll never believe this, Sergeant, but...oh, nothing to report, over. ...I'm comin' in, I don't feel very well."

So now I'm left with the sole question of: how exactly did an alien spider learn how to fly a small helicopter?

Boy, what a conveniently-placed set of watercraft for our heroes and villains to continue their chase with!

How to Run Over a Hobo Without Killing Them: a guide by the Third Doctor.

I'm actually less concerned with how Lupton teleported out of that boat and more concerned with how that plant is moving with no wind.

"...Pretty...!" Looks like Tom wants the crystal now.

I'm seeing this scene with a council of spiders sitting on benches and for some reason I'm having flashbacks to The Puzzle Place.

I think literally the only thing that show had in common with this scene was puppets.

There was a Tumblr post forever ago that said that if Spider-Man's superpower was to shoot spiders at criminals, there would be no crime.

I'm beginning to suspect that's what the Eight Legs' Conquest of Earth plan is: be giant spiders on Earth.

Wow. Tom was so desperate for the crystal that he climbed up a tree to get it.

We just went from "dethroned sales director" to "wants to take over the world" in less than a minute. Lupton, calm the hell down.

Tom actually has a shoebox full of pretty things hidden in a cupboard under the stairs. That's...weirdly sad.

I would call Tom the Beautiful Cinnamon Roll Too Good for This World, Too Pure of this story, but...he did threaten to punch out Yates.

I'll bet Tom was going to give Sarah Jane the crystal, aaaaaand of course now he can't because she needs him to go tell Yates a thing.

OH NO I WAS RIGHT HE WAS GOING TO GIVE HER THE CRYSTAL. Well, this complicates things a bit.

Well at least he was able to pass on the info to Yates and Three.

Looks like they were too late to stop Sarah Jane from getting teleported. Is that Metebelis Three? Kinda looks like the American southwest.

"You speak as if she were alive."
"Yes...yes I do, don't I?"
Aww bless.

I could be wrong, but I think this is the shortest time between arriving on a planet and the locals trying to kill them I've seen.

Huh, from that angle it looks like Three landed in the sky...or maybe he landed RIGHT in front of Sarah Jane.

That...might just be the most ludicrously precise TARDIS landing in all of Classic Who. Sans the returns to the UNIT lab, of course. Ah yes, one last round of Time-Fu with some royal guards before your big exit, Pertwee?

"It's no good! He's dead!"
"He CAN'T be!"
Yeah, we've still got the better part of three episodes to go!

I really hope that bolt isn't what leads to Three's regeneration at the end. Then again, I keep hearing it was "radiation."

Tom's been affected by the crystal? Considering what Three said about it affecting the mind, I wonder what it'll do to him.

He doesn't seem to be having any trouble reading the book anymore. Somehow I saw that coming.

This discussion about whether to attack or not brings me to another burning question: jokes aside, how exactly did the spiders take over?

Was it purely through the use of those crystals? Or are people really just that inherently afraid of spiders?

Of course, now I get to wonder exactly what that machine is supposed to do. Just looks like a lever.

Three I know breakfast is the most important meal of the day but your companion is literally about to be eaten by giant alien spiders.

Actually, I should probably stop calling them "alien" spiders, since they've made it clear that they came from Earth originally.

"Well, now I know what a fly feels like. What an absolutely fascinating experience!" Well I'm glad YOU'RE enjoying this, Three.

When Three said he learned his escape trick from "an old friend," I thought he was talking about Jo at first. But no, it was Houdini.

"Rise, child. You have no reason to fear me, I am your friend." Huh... this was unexpected.

Wait a sec, is that the queen?? This...okay, I have no idea where this is going.

I somehow neglected to bring up bound-and-gagged Yates last time. Nice of them to take that gag off, though.

"I'll help."
"You? Why should you help?"
"Because of Sarah Jane Smith, of course! I want her back just as much as you want Lupton!"
It's lines like this that make me kinda sad that neither of the UNIT boys wound up with anyone in the end.

The Brig and Doris finally got together but Benton and Yates seem to be left as eternal bachelors. ACTUALLY WAIT A SEC THAT'S NOT QUITE TRUE

Wasn't there a novel where Yates turns out to be in a relationship with a man later? #englandforabisexualmikeyates

So for a while I was wondering if Tom had been upgraded to a super-genius or something, but it seems he's just been brought to "normal."

Jury's still out on how I feel about a character with a disability being "cured" by alien magic, though.

Tom seemed perfectly happy just the way he was. It was everyone else at the house who was being a dick to him.

There's a longer discussion to be had about representation of people with disabilities in fiction, but this isn't really the place for it.

But speaking as someone with Asperger's Syndrome, I think I'd rather be understood as a person than "cured."

Okay, personal ramble finished. On with the grand finale of Pertwee!

Tom seems to have Sarah Jane's last words to him on skipping repeat. Or, as we used to call it in the 90s, a remix.

"But why do you want that particular crystal? It's no different from all the others!" I WAS WONDERING WHEN THEY WERE GOING TO BRING THIS UP.

Ah. Apparently that one crystal IS special. "The one last perfect Crystal of Power."

Why do I feel like I can make so many jokes about this, but I can't actually figure one out?

Being psychically forced to march in a circle? Three, I know you're angry but I can think of MUCH worse punishments than this.

I know the spiders can set their phasers to Stun or Kill, so I REALLY hope they're not about to use Kill on Tom.

Sarah Jane is being almost worryingly upbeat and chipper about this escape...

"Tommy, you're normal!" ...You know I was kinda hoping they weren't going to use that word. Oh well.

WAIT A SECOND TOM GOT ZAPPED BUT HE WASN'T
AFFECTED AT ALL?

Ah, this is K'anpo! I've heard of you! And if I remember right, I
think I know how you know the Doctor already.

"You see, I...I found a crystal. A blue crystal."
"'Found'?"
"...Well perhaps 'stole' might be a better word..."

Wow. Okay, maybe Tom isn't a "super-genius" now, but he seems to've
acquired *some* sort of power over the other guys and the spiders.

BECAUSE HE'S LITERALLY JUST STARING AT THEM
RIGHT NOW AND THEY'RE BACKING OFF AND IT'S KIND
OF BADASS

"KILL HIM!" I WAS ALSO NOT EXPECTING THIS TO BE
PERTWEE'S LAST CLIFFHANGER

One of the guys is holding a crowbar...oh my god what did they do.

Aaaaaaand now Sarah Jane is talking with a spider voice and it's kind
of unsettling.

Ohhhh, wait a sec, we've gone back a bit with the other guys. They're
only just now confronting Tom.

"We need more power!" Okay, everybody join fingers...
#byyourpowerscombined #Iamcaptainspider

All this about Three taking the crystal being the catalyst for all this
reminds me that I may be due for a rewatch of The Green Death.
That was one of the first Classic Who serials I watched, and my first
Classic companion departure. Wow, has it really been five years?

"...I know who you are now!"
"You were always a little slow on the uptake, my boy!"
"It's been a long long time."
"You know each other?"
"Oh yes. He was my teacher. My...my guru, if you like...in another
time, in another place."
"Another life!"
"Oh no...don't tell me you're a Time Lord too!"
"I am!"

Wait. I wonder...are they implying that K'anpo is the same guy from the daisiest daisy story? Because that would be pretty cool.

Oooohhhhh this story is bringing together all these tidbits and plot threads from the whole Pertwee era and iT'S SO GREAT.

"Cho-je is a projection of my own self!" ....OKAY THEN.

Wait, are they implying that Three is afraid of spiders or mind control? I thought his big fear was fire because of Inferno?

YATES NO #didsomeonecallforaheroicsacrifice

Jeez, you guys zap an old man in the chest and leave him for dead? Now that's not very zen of you.

Not one of your better perspective shots, I'm afraid, guys. The buildings in the background look about the same size as the TARDIS.

"You will die."
"Well, nevertheless I have to go."
The plot demands it.

Oh. So the locals' attack failed after all. That sucks.

"You have beaten us Doctor. It is good that you will die." Wow. That pause finally made it really sink in that this is Pertwee's last story.

"His compassion protected him, just as Tommy's innocence was his shield." Oh my god. Oh my goooood.

So basically what you're saying is that Tom's pure Cinnamon Roll-ness kept him from getting zapped. Amazing.

AND YATES TOO BECAUSE HE TRIED TO SAVE HIM. HE LITERALLY GOT A PASS ON DEATH BECAUSE HE WANTED TO SAVE SOMEONE ELSE. CAN I HUG EVERYONE.

OH MY GOD BETWEEN YATES AND BENTON AND THREE AND THE METEBELANS IT SEEMS LIKE HALF THIS SERIAL'S CAST IS READY TO DIE WHAT IS HAPPENING D:

omg Yates and Sarah Jane are so cute together but they've only known each other for like two serials or something how did this happen

"I'm afraid this old body has had it, Miss Smith." I was SO SURE he was going to go out on a "this old body is wearing a bit thin."

Oh, looks like he's regenerated into his Cho-je form! I wonder if that makes this the only Doctor Who story with two different regenerations

For a greenscreen set, that sure is a lot of blue.

"I...am...complete!" A sentence I can no longer encounter without hearing it in the Devil's voice from Tenacious D and The Pick of Destiny.

Something that bugs me about this story: it's a great Doctor's grand sendoff, but the villain is just a megalomaniac with no depth.

I mean, Four also died because of a megalomaniac, but that was the Master, and he's special.

Oh well, only six minutes left. Let's do this.

Out with a bang! Let's literally blow up a mountain.

Sarah Jane standing in the lab and hugging Three's check coat is not making this any easier. "He's been gone over three weeks now." Ouch.

"We'll never see him again." *TARDIS noises right on cue*

"Sarah...I got lost in the time vortex...the TARDIS brought me home." Brought him home. BROUGHT HIM HOME CAN WE TALK ABOUT THIS FOR A SECOND

MY FIRST THIRD DOCTOR SERIAL WAS HIS FIRST SERIAL: IT WAS SPEARHEAD FROM SPACE. AND I SPENT THE NEXT YEAR WATCHING ALL THESE SERIALS WHERE THREE WANTED NOTHING MORE BUT TO ESCAPE FROM EARTH. AND NOW IT'S FIVE YEARS LATER AND HE'S ABOUT TO DIE AND HE CALLS EARTH "HOME."

FIVE YEARS. OH MY GOD THAT'S THE LENGTH OF HIS RUN TOO. JON PERTWEE I'M SO GLAD I GOT TO GO ON THIS CRAZY JOURNEY WITH YOU.

"Oh, Doctor, why did you have to go back?"
"I had to face my...my fear, Sarah. I had to face my fear. That was... more important...than just going on living."
"Please...don't die."
"...A tear, Sarah Jane? No, don't cry. While there's life there's............"

I...I seriously don't remember the last time I actually teared up a bit while watching Classic Who.

What a perfect moment for K'anpo to show up looking uncannily like Stephen Colbert. I don't know what else to say.

"Thank you...that makes everything quite clear." Brig. Brig pls.

"He will become a new man."
"Literally?"
"Of course, he will look quite different."
"...Not *again*."

"You may find his behavior somewhat...erratic?" Did...did they just sum up the entire Fourth Doctor era before it even happened.

"Look, Brigadier, look! I think it's starting!"
"Well...here we go again."

Well. I guess that's it then. I've officially completed the entire Jon Pertwee era of Doctor Who. It's been an adventure...

...and Three, Liz, Jo, Sarah Jane, Brig, Benton, Yates, thank you for everything!

And Tom Baker, who I believe is on BBCA as I speak, welcome! You've no idea of the legacy ahead of you.

Originally Posted September 25, 2015

SPEARHEAD FROM SPACE:
REVISITED AND EXTENDED COMMENTARY

I love, LOVE how they transitioned from a black-and-white image of space to a color image of Earth.

Wait a sec, a female UNIT science officer who's not Liz? How come we never learn more about her?

Wait another sec...I don't remember there being FIVE Nestene spheres??

THREE! Hello Three! *whump* well okay then

ALSO HI LIZ

And last but not least, hi Brig! Yeah, I can understand why you didn't find that UNITform terribly flattering.

"I was even searched."
"Security! Rather amusing, don't you think?"
most un-amused glare ever
"No you don't."

Same question I had about five years ago: how exactly did UNIT find Three?

"We used to call him...the Doctor." Believe me, you'll be seeing a loooooooot more of him very shortly.

"Do you want the police told about the police box? They may want it back." That begs another question: when exactly did they get phased out?

I know that police boxes were a normal sight when the show started, but obviously not so much anymore.

Yikes, I kinda feel bad for that x-ray guy. He didn't do anything wrong.

Aaaaaand now I'm becoming suspicious of that surprisingly well-dressed custodian.

Oh, okay. I thought he was going to be a bad guy for a second but nope, he's just out for a quick buck from a newspaper.

"Shoes, must find my shoes..." Three, you're up! And rambling about shoes already.

WOW OKAY it wasn't just one newspaper, apparently it was a whole flock of paparazzi.

I love how Liz Shaw's only expressions in this episode so far have been Pleasantly Bemused and So Done.

Ooooooh crap, that's right, the Brig doesn't know about regeneration yet. This...could prove to be a bit of a problem.

"...Lethbridge-Stewart? My dear fellow, how very nice to see you again." Never mind. Three, you're being surprisingly lucid all of a sudden.

And now the Brig's getting in on this So Done business.

Ah, it seems my suspicions were misplaced. That guy hanging around in the phone booth can't be up to much good.

"Hello! How are you feeling?"
"Shoes."
#iconic

Successfully obtained: shooz.

"Thank you, nurse..."
CHOP TO THE NECK
OKAY HOW DID I COMPLETELY FORGET THAT THREE GETS STRAIGHT-UP ABDUCTED BY CREEPY RANDOS ALTHOUGH I DID REMEMBER THE BEST ESCAPE EVER
#theyseemerollin #theyhatin

BANG "WHO TOLD YOU TO FIRE, YOU STUPID..." wow okay that escalated quickly

Aaaand jump-cut right back to the hospital. Surprise surprise, Three's going to live!

They keep referencing a bullet wound on his head, but they're not actually showing anything. Not even when he actually got shot.

Then again, showing people getting shot in the head is more Pulp Fiction than Doctor Who.

...keeping a potentially alien artifact in a box outside with only one guard doesn't seem like the most practical course of action, guys.

"Something odd about their faces" CUT IMMEDIATELY TO DRAMATIC MUSIC AND SOOTY PLASTIC BABY DOLL FACES WHAT THE ACTUAL CHRIST

Okay I know that might not sound too bad, but that may be the closest thing to a straight-up jump-scare I've seen on Classic Who.

Holy crap, this is like a Halloween special of How It's Made. And not in a fun way.

Everyone's faces is looking surprisingly shiny...and plastic... #dundunduuuun

"We've...changed everything."
"Well I'll say you have!"
Wow, either the Autons work REALLY fast, of they've been here a while already.

Actually, there were the earlier "meteorites" that the Brig mentioned to Liz in the last episode. I'll bet that was the first wave.

Ever so slightly fascinated by the map on the wall. Soviet Union everywhere.

I have a worrying feeling that the ex-partner guy is going to die.

"Am I interrupting?"
"Yes."
"I deal with facts, not with science fiction ideas." Well Miss Shaw, I'm afraid I have some bad news for you...

"No need to get tetchy."
"Well sometimes you can be very aggravating."
Jesus, Brig, chill out, didn't you only just meet her today?

I think I've seen it enough times that I can officially say that Liz Shaw's third expression here is "smug and also kinda terrifying."

I should probably clarify that I don't think Caroline John has a limited range (she certainly doesn't), she just hasn't had much to do yet.

"All energy is a form of life." #theforce

Now how exactly did that Auton make it past the UNIT patrols from earlier?

Ah, thank you Brig for correcting Scobie that Liz Shaw is "not just a pretty face."

Actually, Scobie sounds familiar. I forget, does he show up again in later UNIT stories?

"Where'd that old crate come from?" Wait...wait a sec IS THAT A PRE-PAINTED BESSIE I THINK IT MIGHT BE

Or did Three ask for a roadster "like" that car after this story? I forget, it's been a while.

"Doctors Only" Ahahahahahahaha very clever guys

Wow. I forgot that tub was so fancy. Is that marble? I also forgot that we actually met the red cape's owner, albeit briefly.

Ah yes. Ladies and gentlemen, naked Pertwee in the shower. (although considering the day he's had, he could probably use that shower.)

THAT REMINDS ME. How the hell do I keep forgetting that this came RIGHT off the heels of the end of The War Games??

The Doctor's hasn't just been having a bad day, he's been having a LONG day. Ten episodes of craziness and companion loss and now this?

Of course it's also been long enough since I've seen The War Games that I forget how many days that story took place over.

Aaaaand there's that snake tattoo! Or is that a dragon?

Three, why can't you dry yourself off with the towel you're already weari...oh right.

And so begins the Doctor's noble tradition of stealing post-regeneration clothes from hospitals.

Stealing cars, on the other hand, I think is an exclusively Pertwee thing. Unless you count Matt borrowing a firetruck in The Eleventh Hour.

"...That's odd."
"Wrong key."
I'm beginning to wish that Big Finish had gotten to a season 7 UNIT spin-off before Caroline John passed.

WOAH THAT'S A LOT OF BLOOD FOR THIS SHOW. That also might explain why that UNIT officer wasn't featured in any future stories.

"Alright, alright I supposed you want to see my pass? Yes well I haven't got one. And I'm not going to tell you my name either! Well you just tell Brigadier Lethbridge-Stewart that I want to see him. Well don't just stand there arguing with me man, get on with it!"

.........wait a sec since when does the Doctor have a TARDIS-homing wristwatch.

"Very flexible, you know. Could be useful on the planet Delphon where they communicate with their eyebrows."

"You arrived last night in a shower of meteorites." Ah, so it has been a day. Also, that looked like a pretty sunlit night.

Okay Three and Liz literally just met a minute ago and they're already being super adorable together how did that happen.

Ohhhhhh no, Scobie's not unknowingly having an Auton made of him, is he?

But first: makeshift crowbars and break-ins! And does a doll factory really need barbed wire over its walls?

Ah, haven't had a good cliffhanger face-mug for a while.

I DO NOT REMEMBER THE AUTONS BEING ABLE TO RUN

Frankly, I'm amazed that guy made it out of there alive.

"Auto Plastics" Aahahahahaha very clever guys: the sequel.

Wow, he didn't just make it out alive, he made it to UNIT and I'll bet he's going to give Three and Liz the missing pieces of the puzzle.

If he can speak coherently again, that is.

"PRIMITIVE? We've got lasers…" omg why does that crack me up. It's the 70s! WE'VE GOT LASERS!!

"What we need is a…lateral molecular rectifier."
"What on earth's that?"
"Not on Earth, unfortunately."

Oh. Hang on, I thought that was the UNIT officer who died in the crash. I guess that was someone else.

Dr. Elizabeth Shaw: scientist, master of over a dozen subjects, part-time petty thief. Lady's got talent. #getthattardiskey

Yikes, the TARDIS is looking pretty shabby at this angle. Doesn't sound too well either.

"Doctor, you tricked me." Oh my god the Brig and Liz are like Three's angry parents ready to give him a good scolding.

he's being so sheepish too oh man this is great.

"Give me the key, Doctor."
"…Must I?"

Seeley, this really REALLY isn't the time to be bargaining with UNIT. Then again, I don't think there IS ever a good time.

Okay, I distinctly remember Seeley's wife doesn't die, but that doesn't make this any less unsettling.

I ALSO FORGOT THAT SHE WAS ARMED WITH A FREAK-ING RIFLE.

Well at least they spared us a scene of the Auton knocking her out.

"Destroy! Total destruction!" WOW OKAY I REALLY SHOULD'VE GUESSED THAT "TOTAL" MEANT "EVAPORATE THE BODY" BUT SOMEHOW I DIDN'T

Aaaaaand they finally make it to the factory and Channing is just. standing there. watching them. like three inches away. Not creepy at all.

"Our new line is display mannequins for shops, we send them all over the country." #OHSHIT

oh god is Scobie going to open the door and find the Auton double of him THAT IS EXACTLY WHAT HAPPENED OH MY GOD

Didn't mention this before for some reason, but I think this is the only Pertwee story with a zooming title card.

"If we can establish the frequency on which it operates..."
BANG
"Oh dear."
"...We overloaded the circuit, I think."

As authoritarian as the Brig usually is, it's actually quite fun to see him rage against the system like this.

"I think all that group are top civil servants." Right across from the US presidents. Madame Tussauds, you may have your priorities mixed.

Said the young lady who isn't entirely sure what exactly a civil servant is.

"Doctor, what are you doing?" Yeah, the plastic probably doesn't smell that good, Three.

Wait. So did Auton!Scobie steal the real ones' watch, or did it kill the real Scobie and somehow put his body on display?

OH MY GOD WHAT IF THREE WAS SNIFFING FOR THE SMELL OF PLASTIC OR HUMAN FLESH

I'm usually not prudish about this stuff but uh, yeah, the Nestene Consciousness kinda does look like something you'd want to keep covered by your pants.

I keep forgetting this UNIT officer's name is Captain Munro. I do have to wonder why we never saw him again? I hope he doesn't die.

wait do the fire extinguishers seriously say "waterloo" on them

Also SCOBIE'S DOUBLE WAS AT THE UNIT LAB WHICH
MEANS THE SCOBIE IN THE MUSEUM *IS* THE REAL
SCOBIE'S CORPSE

How is it so easy to forget just how effing terrifying the Autons really
are?

Pay no attention to the Doctor and Liz behind the curtain.

"Only dummies...I think." Thanks, Three, that's reassuring.

I WAS RIGHT ABOUT THE STANDING CORPSE OH GOD

"Where are they going?"
"To take their places."
Oh no. That's why Liz said that they were all government types.

I DO NOT WELCOME THESE NEW PLASTIC OVERLORDS

Ah, a peaceful London morning. Not a soul about, shop window
dummies preparing to straight up murder everyone...

Ah yes, that one guy who dies by somersaulting forward. #doabar-
relroll

"We have been colonizing other planets for a thousand million years."
That's...that's a lot of years.

An unfortunate end for Hibbert, but at least he died doing the right thing.

Oh! So the real Scobie wasn't dead after all! That's nice. All those
museum patrons sound pretty freaked out about him coming to life
though

And so begins another noble tradition of UNIT encountering
bulletproof aliens and being able to do nothing but pump lead.

"Good gracious. What on earth is this thing?" I'm feeling less prudish now so...it's a butthole in a box.

"Is that what you look like on your own planet?" I SHOULD HOPE
NOT

And...and now it's sprouted tentacles. This, um...well then.

Ah, the day is saved thanks to Liz Shaw and her quick techno-fiddling!

"And there's that car, too. Yes, I took to that car. I'd like to have it!"
"No, Doctor. That car must be returned to its owner."
"Must it? Yes, yes I suppose it must. Still, there's no reason why you couldn't find me something similar, is there?"
BESSIE!

"Good! When can we go and choose it?" omg humanity nearly ended and Three just wants to go car shopping why is this adorable

"By the way, I just realized: I don't even know your name."
"Smith. Doctor John Smith."

And on that note, UNIT Era aweeeeeiiiiiigh!!!

Huh. I could've sworn there was one more scene with Seeley and his wife. Or maybe I was thinking of a different serial.

In Loving Memory of Caroline John

CHARACTER RETROSPECTIVE:
UNIT

Usually I wait to include a Character Retrospective until after their last major appearance on the show, but for UNIT I'll make an exception. Considering UNIT is arguably best known for the Third Doctor era, it seems most appropriate that I include them in this volume instead of after the Doctor's departure from UNIT at the beginning of Four's era, or even after the last Classic Who UNIT story with "Battlefield." So let's kick things off with the main man himself: Brigadier Alistair Gordon Lethbridge-Stewart. No supporting character has had quite the longevity throughout the series as the Brig has had. He's been onscreen with five of the eight Classic Doctors (Two, Three, Four, Five, and Seven), and most of those remaining gaps have since been filled by Big Finish with *The Spectre of Lanyon Moor* (Six) and *Minuet in Hell* (Eight). Even after Nicholas Courtney's death, his legacy lived on in New Who with name-drops, a plot-altering phone call in "The Wedding of River Song," and finally culminating in the introduction of the Brig's daughter, Kate Stewart.

So what made the character such a mainstay? I think there are two main factors. First, the Brig is a foil for the Doctor in a way that his usual companions are not. Considering Three is a much more action-oriented Doctor, a dapper badass like the Brig should feel like a redundant character...but he really isn't. They're both on the same side, but the Doctor is a man of science and reason, whereas the Brig is a military mind. He frequently shoots and asks questions later and often believes that the best solution to a problem is "blow it up," but he's still undeniably one of the good guys. Soldiers tend to get a bad rap on *Doctor Who*, and the Brig is certainly not immune to the Doctor's criticism, but there still exists a certain (albeit sometimes begrudging) mutual respect between the two. Especially with the Third Doctor. The Brig knows that the scope of the Doctor's knowledge far exceeds his own, and the Doctor knows that the Brig is always committed to getting the job done. Second, the Brig became the Doctor's anchor to Earth. Five whole seasons with one organization as your home base will probably do that to you. It's interesting to see how even when the Brig is exasperated by the Doctor's antics, he's still grateful to have him around. Even when they've spent considerable time apart in later seasons, they're pleased to see each other again. The Doctor's bodies come and go, but the camaraderie remains.

Speaking in terms of the general scheme of UNIT, I find it kind of fascinating that our three central men are all at very different ranks. Still, they seem to form a loose Head, Hand, and Heart trinity that gives them a certain sense of balance. The Brig is, of course, the Head: the man at the top, the one who knows what to do and gives all the orders. Benton and Yates both embody certain aspects of the Hand (the fighter on the ground, the action man) and the Heart (the emotional center, the compassionate one), but if I had to pick one for each, I would probably say that Yates is the Hand and Benton is the Heart. Benton and Yates both have their cute moments with Jo and Sarah Jane, but Benton seems to be the more consistently good-natured. He smiles more, he tries his best to be in the good graces of others, and he has a more open sense of humor. He's the UNIT officer you wouldn't mind bringing home to meet your parents. On the other hand, he can be very self-sacrificing when the situation calls for it, and isn't afraid to get into a tussle with just about anyone.

Which brings me to Yates. I talked a bit about his relationship with Jo in her retrospective, so I won't be a broken record about it here. Unlike Benton, Yates is given something more resembling a character arc. Unusual for *Doctor Who*, it's not a progression of the character becoming a better person (such as is the case for many companions), but instead is a subtle build-up to a rapid downward spiral that causes him to crash, from which he must put himself together again. To the best of my knowledge, the closest thing we've seen to that elsewhere in the TV show is Clara's arc in season 8 of New Who, where she becomes gradually more deceptive of her friends and loved ones. When I first heard about Yates' betrayal in "Invasion of the Dinosaurs," I thought it came a little out of nowhere. But when I watched it, the set-up made sense. Despite his action-man exterior, Yates does have a sensitive side that has nothing to do with romantic pursuits. He wants to be at peace with himself and comfortable in the world he lives in. At the very least, he has no lack of good company in the cozy atmosphere of the UNIT Family. Yates has interesting dynamics with all of the characters, from his loving rapport with Jo to his alternating good-chums/superior-officer relationship with Benton to his not-always-complete loyalty to the Brig. And that's a big part of what makes UNIT as a whole work: it's a weird sort of family that has very different ways of loving each other. Sometimes it's willing to risk your life for someone else, sometimes it's just being there when someone comes back after a long time away, even if they look a lot different.

CHARACTER RETROSPECTIVE: THE THIRD DOCTOR

The introduction of any new Doctor is going to come with its challenges. It was asked of Hartnell, "can you make this show work in the first place?" and it was asked of Troughton, "can you keep the show going?" Of Pertwee it was asked, "can you carry the show in mostly one location?" Also, "will the audience accept an action hero Doctor?" The answers seem to be, yes and yes. Jon Pertwee is a Doctor who kicks some serious ass, and the fact that they were able to strike a balance between this and the Doctor's usual mind-over-matter approach to conflict resolution is quite impressive. Three gets a physical combat style that involves disabling opponents more than outright harming them (although I image that happens as well). Even when he's being violent, he's still being peaceful in a sense; quite a feat for an ostensibly stir-crazy Doctor.

Three is also the first Doctor who gets to be, dare I say it, suave. He gets a winning combination of stylish vintage outfits, a debonair demeanor, James-Bond-like competence in action scenes, a taste for fine wines, and lest we forget that shower scene in "Spearhead from Space" (unless I'm mistaken, we don't get something like that again until Donna meets the Tenth Doctor's hand-clone in "Journey's End"). Also, let's just say I've seen more than one post about Three from the Classic Who Tumblr community of the "oh Doctor, what a tight shirt you're wearing" variety. Taking this a step further, I would argue that Three is the first Doctor to have significant chemistry with a female companion. Not that One and Two didn't care for theirs, because they certainly did, but I feel like the fact that Jo meets a man whom she describes as "a younger [Third] Doctor" and then ends up marrying him says a lot about her relationship with Three. He and Jo obviously loved each other very much, although how much of that was actually romantic is still up for debate. I personally read it as 90% platonic/10% Jo had a crush on Three.

Speaking of love, let's talk about Three and his favorite planet. Something that surprisingly works about keeping the Doctor on Earth for an extended period is that it's still able to create conflict, and not just in the monster-of-the-week sense. As much as the Doctor loves Earth, Three is rarely complacent in his exile and clashes with his superiors, sometimes even his friends. He's also the first Doctor to be shown to have superiors at all, unless you count the Time Lords appearing at the very end of Troughton's run. A fascinating contrast, when you consider that Three is one of the most openly anti-authoritarian Doctors, with Four as a close second. How does the Doctor deal with having A Boss? Not always terribly well, it seems. Still, Three's general disdain for military minds ultimately doesn't keep him from seeing the good in individuals; I highly doubt the Brigadier would have become such a vital and beloved character in the Whoniverse if it had.

As stated in my introduction, I tend to cite Three as my favorite Classic Doctor. I think the reason why is something of a "Goldilocks and the Three Bears" answer. The Third Doctor is, for me, "just right" in most respects of what makes the Doctor the Doctor. Just the right amount of alien, just the right amount of humanity, just the right amount of dashing heroics, just the right amount of pacifism, just the right amount of disdain, just the right amount of love, just the right amount of mistrust of authority, and just the right amount of pal-i-ness with his companions. So much about him balances out. Pertwee's performance delivers a perfect blend of nonchalance and frustration, peace and anger, fun and business. Despite the whole regeneration process, the Third Doctor does seem to have kept his predecessor's face: by which I mean, Pertwee's face is just as delightfully elastic as Troughton's and it's an absolute joy to watch. Equally nice to watch is Three's gradual softening over the course of his tenure, not unlike One. Three begins with a love-hate relationship with Earth and its people throughout season 7, but by the end of "Planet of the Spiders" has come to call it "home." This makes it a bit of a shame that he comes to this conclusion minutes before regenerating into a Doctor who hightails it from Earth pretty quickly. Then again, the Doctor had to return to all of time and space sooner or later.

ABOUT THE AUTHOR

Hannah J. Rothman is an American Whovian who came to the party a little late. By the time she started watching *Doctor Who*, the 2009 specials were well underway and by the time she was officially a fan, the Tenth Doctor was pleading "I don't want to go." She spent the following year (particularly that summer) soaking up as much Classic Who as humanly possible, drawing fan art, contributing to the fanzine *The Terrible Zodin*, developing preposterous amounts of head-canon for the Fifth Doctor and his original trio of sadly underdeveloped companions, and making some wonderful friends in the fandom online. There was also a lot of Tweeting. Hannah sports a BA in English and currently lives in bustling New York City, where she has thankfully never encountered any Daleks on the Empire State Building. Her other geeky writing can be found in *Outside In 1* and *2*, and *Chicks Dig Gaming*.

Connect with Hannah online:

Website: http://hannahjrothman.com

Want to watch the Tweets as they happen? Join me at https://twitter.com/WhoBlogLiveFeed

Join the discussion! Visit the original blog archive at http://classicwhoblog.livejournal.com/

TWITTER WHO VOLUME 1:
THE FIRST DOCTOR

**A journey of a hundred serials begins with a single tweet.
Okay, more than 100.**

Whofolk, you are hereby invited to the first chapter of an epic quest as one lone fan traverses the vast realm of Classic Who through fresh eyes: a fan born...wait for it...after 1989. The journey ahead is long and intricate and she wields one tool to document it: Twitter. Bursting from the pages of *Outside In,* Hannah J. Rothman returns to the beginning as she Tweets and commentates her way through the complete William Hartnell era of *Doctor Who.* Grab your lapels and get your sonics ready.

TWITTER WHO VOLUME 2:
THE SECOND DOCTOR

**There are some corners of the universe which have bred
the most wonderful things. They must be Tweeted!**

The race to the end of the '60s is one filled with gaping holes, holes that are being reconstructed. Want to come along with Hannah on this next leg of her journey? She's set down 140 more planks for you, you'll be perfectly safe. Hannah J. Rothman continues her epic quest to Tweet her way through Classic *Doctor Who* as she tackles the complete Patrick Troughton era, recons and all. Includes the commentary for the "Marcr Terror," originally printed in *Outside In.* Grab your favorite Highlander and get your sonics ready.

Available in print and ebook at all the usual places.

www.ingramcontent.com/pod-product-compliance
Lightning Source LLC
Chambersburg PA
CBHW060919040426

42445CB00011B/698